Just Ask

Emily Thayer Guziak

This book is memoir. This book does not claim to convey *the* truth. It reflects the author's present recollections of experiences over time. Some names and characteristics have been changed, some events have been compressed, and some dialogue has been recreated. Some of the material has appeared in *Traverse, Northern Michigan's Magazine.*

This book includes words which today are considered offensive, ethnic slurs. In some cases, I recall conversations which truly were offensive at the time. In other cases, I recall conversations in which those speaking were not aware the term would soon be considered offensive. I use the terms to retain the authenticity of my life. I apologize for any offense to the reader.

ISBN (paperback): 978-0-578-32722-8
ISBN (ebook): 978-0-578-98529-9

Book design by Christy Day, Constellation Book Services
www.constellationbookservices.com

Printed in the United States of America

To my father, Bruce William Thayer

Prologue

When I am growing up in the Chicago suburb of Winnetka, it is a bucolic place.

Perfect, really, in the minds of many of its wealthy inhabitants, because in this little village of 12,000 people nestled on about four square miles, some of it along Lake Michigan, there are public servants to regulate most everything. Thus, by all appearances, this affluent enclave is perfect. In 1955 when my parents choose to purchase a small, white brick, thirty-five-year-old home for $10,000 cash in—naturally, an all-white, nearly all-Protestant neighborhood, they take a step towards my mother's goal of country club life and lock my father into a life I'm just not sure he wanted.

I don't blame my mother, who, like my dad, grew up in nearby Evanston, attended the massive Evanston Township High School, and went east to college. Their upwardly mobile step into Winnetka—in 1954—marked Greatest Generation success. The Winnetka Public Schools with its progressive education, attracted them. Ironically, it is a school system where I will thrive in my friendships and fail miserably in their progressive math.

But I believe Dad needed an escape to something else—acreage maybe—where he could raise fruit trees and piss in the bushes and let my sister and me, and my brother, roam bare chested.

This, anyway, is how I choose to explain why my dad had a hard time playing the part of the white, upper-middle-class dad; a reason why I feel he held back unconditional love. And this is my story; the story of how Dad and I try to unleash the love between a father and a daughter.

INTRODUCTION

Some thirty-five years ago, I took a creative writing workshop at the University of Vermont.

It was an evening class, not for credit, and most likely intended for just what I needed: a chance to express myself while working to support myself.

I'd been told six months earlier, at a very expensive, month-long fiction-writing workshop that I had some talent, but investment in an MFA was needed if I was to ever successfully write creatively.

I was much too scared to leap head first into that unknown world, so I wrote a book while working.

It took a long time to complete this book; I was happily waylaid by marriage, babies, child-rearing, travel, friends, weddings, and memorial services.

At that workshop in 1987, the teacher asked us to draw a picture with colored markers of what our writing looks like, to us. In my spiral-bound notebook, without hesitation, I aggressively scribbled the licking flames of a fire in bright shades of orange, red and blue.

My writing is a fire that burns inside me.

This book is my ever-burning fire.

CHAPTER ONE
"Seeking"

"Is it Wednesday?" Wednesday is A&P day, and the night sometimes Dad doesn't come home for dinner. Mom is draining her coffee cup and hanging up the phone, so I know it is time to do something. I'd been chasing specks of dust floating in afternoon rays of sunshine, seemingly dancing in my soft-as-butter corduroy overalls near the bay windows of our living room, bright patches of sunlight checkering our worn, chocolate-hued carpet.

"Yep. And we're in a hurry to get Betsy to choir on time." Betsy has choir practice at our church in Evanston every Wednesday, which is a dark, scary place I hate but where we hafta go on Sundays. Every Sunday.

I take my faded red play jacket from its plastic hook in the under-the-stairs closet and shrug into it, my fingers crossed. "Is it Mary's Cupboard tonight?" I ask, thinking that if it is, I'll start deciding between a milkshake at dinner or an Eskimo Pie from White's Drugstore on the way home. Mom is outlining her lips with Bonnie Bell Shell Pink and rubbing them together like Robbie does, when he smells cookies at my Aunt Ginny's house. She is my fun aunt who is very, very skinny and hugs Uncle Tom all the time and makes her oatmeal cookies every time we go over.

"Not tonight. It's pork chops tonight."

With pork chops comes applesauce, and I like that, so I can cross dinner off my Worry List and not think about Dad coming home. I just gotta remember the "Don't-Talk-About-List" so Mom will be happy. The list includes No Talking About:

New shoes from Voses, even though getting new shoes is about the best thing that can happen because I am happy the whole time I am in the store. I smell all the leather shoes, and the man who looks kinda like Dad smiles and measures my foot and tries lotsa shoes on me and then gives me a Safe-T-Pop.

Robbie, who is 7 and three years older than me, doing glitter-painting on the table yesterday where Betsy's and my dollhouse is, and making the table all glittery.

Betsy sneaking Trix cereal into her bedroom when Dougie from next door gave it to her. We only get Grape-Nuts and Shredded Wheat.

Getting in trouble in Jeff's bedroom when I tried on his blue jeans because I want to be a boy SO BAD. I think I want this cuz Dad likes boy stuff, not girl stuff.

Robbie putting the red sticker that says "Nixon's the One," which he got from Uncle George, on his desk chair.

"*Do not,*" Mom says as she hands two ten dollar bills to the A&P clerk an hour later, "tell your father how much I spent." She accepts her change from the polyester-uniformed clerk, and clasps shut the black purse hanging from her arm. "He'll be tired tonight."

Clutching my oblong tube of Oscar Mayer liver sausage, I add this to my "Don't-Talk-About" List and squeeze my four-year-old body a little ball into the very back space of Mom's Volkswagen; I am only allowed to sit in this special little hold on the drive home from the A&P. It is my treat for hurrying in the grocery store. Mom likes to hurry, I think, because we always hurry.

Deep down in my heart, squished into a tiny ball, are my secret feelings.

Sometimes at night, after I say "Nancy's Prayer" that my grandfather wrote, and I bless a bunch of people, I tell my secret feelings to God. My biggest secret is that I want a dad like Beaver has on the TV show *Leave it To Beaver*, because then I'd always know my dad loves me. My other secret is I want to be Beaver, because I need to be a boy. I just know Dad would love me if I am a boy, and also, I wouldn't have to wear dresses.

I tell God that I really want to be Beaver because his dad looks right at him and worries when Beaver is in trouble. I don't know if my dad loves me. I guess he does, because he goes to work all the time and he doesn't yell. But he never says stuff like, "I guess that made you feel pretty badly,

Beaver," and he doesn't look at me very much. Beaver's dad, called Ward, looks at Beaver all the time.

I think my own dad just doesn't know how to show that he loves me, like he never learned.

The other reason I want to be Beaver is that his Mom's never in a hurry. But mostly because his dad loves him.

> "You know June, we'd be a lot better parents if we didn't wait until they did something good to let them know we're proud of them. Every once in a while, for just no reason at all, we oughta tell them we love them."
>
> Ward to June in "The Musician," season 1, episode 30.

I have an explicit memory that, when I was an infant, Dad didn't want to hold me.

I am messy, squirmy; I pee and I cry. When he does, on the few occasions he must assume that responsibility, his arms stiffen as I am placed in them by Mom, and my lithe, relaxed little body becomes as rigid as his broad chest muscles. He is athletic, a lover of the outdoors, and a highly disciplined man who does Royal Canadian Air Force exercises every evening.

Yet we are all instinctive creatures and so I think, at two years old as I wrap my skinny little toddler arms around his neck to hold on, that he has to love me.

Dad is a phenomenal salesman who will make lots of money. I will benefit from that. But I believe that he never told me he loved me when I was a child, a college student or in my twenties, struggling to find his love through a myriad of messy, break-all-the-rules relationships.

I believe he was actually a scared little boy so very fearful of loving, this mountain of a man, massive and scary to me, a toddler.

Dad is tall with jet-black hair, long legs that only my sister Betsy will inherit, and skin perpetually tanned by the sun. His brown eyes are large and expressive, coming from his mother's Harrison genes. The trait must have come into the WASPish family gene pool through a long-ago Latin lover.

His words are few; this will cause me, for many years into my marriage, to try to yank thoughts from my husband's mind when he pauses reflectively. To me, no words from a man I want to love means no feelings.

But what a bunch of blundering between me and my dad, until the scared little boy and the perpetual runaway daughter can circle the corral, rein in their horses, and say we love each other.

When Dad gets home from work, when I am young, mostly I am so hungry I just want him to hurry up and drink his brown stuff with ice cubes, with Mom, so we can eat. I am supposed to play in the yard or watch cartoons with Robbie, but it is always Clutch Cargo on TV that Robbie makes us watch. There's no mom on the show, and I don't like it.

Most important at my house on Fairview Avenue are rules, especially when Dad is home. Mom Rules are OK. I can be Me with Mom Rules because the worst one—wearing the dumb, ugly dress that itches to church—is a quick one. The second worst one, only two cookies after lunch even if they're my very favorite kind—chocolate marshmallow, which I can pretend is a 3 Musketeers bar that we can't have—you kinda get used to.

But Dad Rules make me feel like I'm not me, but instead have a stern"do-what-you-least-want-to-do-when-you-least-want-to-do-it" value that trails me into my young adulthood so strongly that it takes a boyfriend threatening a break-up unless I agree to join him and others for brunch on a Saturday before household chores, to change.

Dad Rules are cold, mean, scary, and way too hard to follow.

Why does Dad have kids if he wants so many rules?

> "Well, I guess I made a mistake, Beaver. I guess that I was so anxious to be right that I ... I kind of forgot what it felt like when I was a little boy,"
>
> Ward to Beaver, "Party Invitation," season 1, episode 15.

"He's here!" Mom grabs her tan cardigan off the back of the kitchen chair and hurries to the front door. "Bruce, he's here."

Dad comes out of the bathroom, sliding a small black comb into his back pocket. "I'll be outside," he says, and steps into the kitchen to grab a dish towel and walks out the back door.

I am perched in front of our TV, a rare treat on a Sunday afternoon. It is the only way Mom knows how to keep me from getting dirty on a summer day. I clutch my favorite stuffed dog, Woof, and try to lose myself in the jerky motions of Davey and Goliath on the TV screen as they face yet another moral challenge.

"Betsy, get your sister." Mom opens the screen door to my Uncle George. "Thanks so much, George," Mom says and reaches up to straighten the round collar of her white blouse over her sweater. My Uncle George has come over to take a picture of all of us in front of Dad's new car.

"It's a beaut," Uncle George grins and waves to me. He is my uncle that always smiles. They live just three blocks away, and Carol, my cousin, comes to my birthday parties. "I'll go help Bruce."

The brand-new light green station wagon gleams in the summer sun where Dad has parked it on the driveway, and a canopy of green from the trees serves as a background. I clutch Woof and walk outside with Betsy, feeling strange in a dress on a Sunday afternoon, but Mom says I can't change until after the picture. "Don't pull out your bangs," Betsy says to me. "Just 'til the picture's done," she adds, refastening the yellow plastic barrette anchoring back her own brown bangs.

I stand with both hands firmly around Woof's neck. Robbie, behind me in a collared shirt and shorts, grins happily and my sister, sporting a seersucker dress identical to mine, looks into Uncle George's camera as if it's just another photo op.

When I look at the photo now, I see Dad, at 37 years old, standing straight and tall with his new car behind him, the sun glinting off the windows, and his family in front of him. His plaid sports shirt is neatly tucked into his shorts and a gold watch gleams on his wrist. Mom looks as if she forgot to run a comb through her hair, but she has gathered her chicks and done her job.

I wonder, now, did we run back to our toys after the photo was taken? Did Dad keep polishing the car's silver chrome with the dish towel, or did we all tumble in for a ride around the block? I look at the photo and think how happy we look—how 1950s suburban normal. Yet inside I am scared of the tall man in the plaid shirt. What was he most proud of; the gleaming new car or his family?

"Do NOT go back in the sand." I shiver as I cling to Dad's neck—I am dripping wet and water is in my eyes because he has dunked me several times in Lake Michigan to rid me of tiny sand particles, and the greasy remnants of Ski & Sea lotion. It is a Sunday afternoon, during summer vacation. The white criss-crossed straps of my red bathing suit cut into my sunburned shoulders as he lifts me with stiff arms to Mom on the concrete pier of Elder Lane Beach. I watch as he swishes and dunks Robbie back and forth too; then Robbie is hoisted up, and we run up the stone steps to the playground, beach towels flapping over our shoulders.

The metal slide is burning hot on my legs as I try to slide down in my still-wet bathing suit, and my thin, yellow rubber flip-flops fall off my feet as I jump off the end. "Dad said no," I singsong as Robbie runs off the grass and onto the swings that are anchored in the sandy part of the playground. "Underdog push. I dare ya," Robbie always wants company in his rebellions. I am always a more-than-willing partner; I crave attention from either of my siblings. "Plus, ya owe me," Robbie says.

I push against the elastic waistband of Robbie's bathing suit and time my underdog push so I will not be caught by his legs. He is smiling, this risk-taking brother of mine, as Dad crests the stairs, a wicker basket with its cork-capped Thermos and remnants of peanut butter sandwiches hoisted onto his shoulder.

I see his tanned legs, his feet in his brown and blue flip-flops and his red plaid bathing suit and wonder if maybe, just maybe, he will smile and remember how good it feels to put your bare feet in sun-drenched sand and run through its squishy surface while you give your big brother an underdog push.

Or, if my father would just yell at us about our sandy feet and going against his order, then maybe I could cry and Robbie could tell him that a clean car is a stupid rule and maybe we could talk a little and we—this upper, middle class family in Winnetka—could feel some emotion rather than emptiness because Dad's stony stare and brusque rewashing of our feet only makes me think I have failed once again to earn his love.

"Uh-uh," is all Dad says when we do something that in his eyes is wrong. From an early age I must figure out what he wants from me because there are so few words. Now, there must be no sand on us when we get in the car, and even though Dad leaves the new car in the garage and drives the Volkswagen Bug to the beach, it makes no difference.

No dirt allowed in the cars.

I walk across the parking lot. My feet make squishing sounds in my wet flip-flops and I sit in the middle of the backseat of the hot car on a folded towel. It is less than five minutes to drive home, but it can seem much longer when you can't touch a car window or poke your big brother in the stomach.

"Floor pads," Dad says when we pull in the driveway. Betsy and Robbie reach down to straighten the rubber mats underneath their feet, and Dad checks the windows for fingerprints. This is our routine.

"Why can't we stop, Dad?" I ask, on a weekend car trip.

"We'll stop when we need gas," Dad says, and I curl myself into a tiny ball in the back seat, as best I can with a seat belt on, hoping that Mom convinces him to stop sooner.

"I have gum," Mom says from the front seat, reaching into her purse for the slim green package of sugarless gum. It is another Sunday afternoon, and we have been driving for a long time, returning from a weekend trip to Canada. I am very hungry. I am allowed my *Leave It to Beaver* coloring book and a small box of crayons, but coloring in the car gives me a headache. I accept a slice of Mom's gum, its powder leaving a trace on my fingers. It tastes a little funny, this Amurol gum, but the sweet saliva going down to my tummy makes me a little less hungry. It is all that is allowed in the car, and though Mom will sing songs and play the alphabet game, I'm still hungry and have to go to the bathroom and don't understand why Dad hates to stop or why there are No Snacks allowed.

Mom will explain this away, when I am older, by saying that Dad loved the order of the military during his two years with the US Navy, from 1943-45, and that he is happiest when all is in order.

But people are never in order, especially kids.

Poor Dad.

> "Boy Dad, are you and Mom admitting that sometimes you make mistakes?" Beaver asks Ward.
>
> "Yeah Beaver, I guess I am. Sometimes we lay it on pretty heavy."
>
> "Beaver Won't Eat," season 4, episode one.

The year I am eight, Halloween is finally on a Saturday, which means trick-or-treating past bedtime. It is also the first Halloween where I get to make my own costume and not wear the Little Red Devil jumpsuit with "Glitter Glo" horns and its hard plastic mask that Betsy talked Mom into buying it at Woolworths in Evanston all the way back when she was in kindergarten.

I get to dress up as a hobo and my best friend, Allison,

has promised to pick me up for trick or treating, as soon as it begins to get dark. Winnetka has lots and lots of streets with big sidewalks and we never run out of houses. Unless we walk four blocks to Lake Michigan. Then the houses end. But we don't go there because those houses have really long driveways.

"Just don't go as far as Sheridan Road," Mom says.

"Why?" All I know about the houses on Sheridan Road is that they have really long driveways. And some senator lives over there.

"We don't know anyone over there, so it's not polite to go trick or treating there. So just stay closer to home," she says.

What my mom doesn't mention to us is that an unsolved murder occurred a month ago, in a home on Sheridan Road.

"Ya gotta be ready!"

Allison flicks dirty blond bangs out of her eyes and glances quickly at me from her Slap Jack game with Wendy. It is chilly on this Halloween afternoon, and the cold from her wide concrete front steps seeps through our jeans. Wendy slaps a jack and grins; Allison gives me her "can-you-believe it?" smile—the smile we have shared since junior kindergarten. It is the smile that bonds me and Allison against the world, and sends a warm, squishy feeling from my tummy to my heart.

"We gotta get to a lot of houses, so be ready for us at six!"

"Us?" I ask, rising and starting down the steps.

"Yeah, Wendy's coming too. She's eating dinner here, first."

My warm, squishy feeling goes away. I feel my hands getting hot, and a hard beat, beat, beat in my heart that hurts.

I run through Allison's yard to the corner and cross onto my street. I only have to pass the MacGregor's big, wide side yard, and then I am home.

Wendy is new. She is in Allison's class at Greeley, and not mine. Allison has been playing with Wendy a lot, I think, because her brother has a drum set in his bedroom and cuz her mom lets you eat cookies anywhere in the house. Whenever I tell Mom that Allison likes Wendy better than me, she says I'm being silly.

"You shouldn't feel that way," she says and goes back to whatever Mom thing she is doing. She says that at least a thousand times a week.

Mom says I am in Mrs. Mustoe's third grade class with different girls because they like to mix you up. "It's a good social skill to learn to make new friends," she says. I only know that it means I don't get to see Allison except walking home at lunch.

The tight, scrunchy feeling I get in my stomach when I see Allison and Wendy together is the same one I get when Dad doesn't smile. Or when he asks who left the light on upstairs, when we finally get to sit down at the dining room table and he says we can't eat 'til someone turns it off.

So I always turn it off. 'Cuz I want to eat. And I am scared of Dad.

"Your turn for Dad's car, ya know." Robbie, in our front yard, looks up from his purple Schwinn bike. "He's home."

Every Saturday is Car Cleaning, and Betsy and Robbie and I take turns. Car cleaning is dumb and gross and we hate it. But it is a rule. Another stupid rule.

"Is he in a good mood?" I ask Robbie.

"Dunno. He just made me sweep the garage over again. Twice. I'm outa here." Robbie flies down the driveway on his new ten-speed, off for parts of Winnetka he never visited with me, when he was way younger and rode me around on the back of his banana bike.

I gotta have time to rip up Robbie's old pants and put charcoal all over my face, to look dirty, for my hobo costume.

The tan Buick sedan is in the driveway, and I take the little whisk broom out of the glove compartment and start sweeping tiny pieces of stupid dirt off the tan carpet. Every time I brush the skinny little husks over the floor, I get all tight in my shoulders and I feel mean inside, like I want to yell at Annie, who lives across the street and is only six, and I can boss around.

Dad's inspection is worse than the work. Every Saturday Dad gets weird about the dumb cars.

"I found a dime. It could've been yours."

Dad is bent at the waist, sweeping with the whisk broom in the corners of the back-seat floor of the Buick. His voice is so muffled I can hardly hear him.

I stare at Dad's broad back and then look up at the stone path leading to the front door. All I care about is being ready when Allison picks me up. I don't even care about the dime that Dad found instead of me, even though I could take two more cents from my bank and buy a new Dennis the Menace comic book after school next week.

"Why does it have to be so clean?" I whine. "I gotta go Dad. It's Halloween." I stretch out the word Halloween really, really long so he'll maybe get that it's a big deal. I thrust my hands into the pockets of my jeans.

"Because, I said so," he says.

"Dad, lemme go inside and get ready to go with Allison." I want to look like the hobos we sing about in Miss Haight's music class at Greeley School. We sing "This Land is your Land" and she tells us the writer was a hobo who was poor.

Dad twists the upper half of his body out from the inside of the car. He turns, and sorta smiles, but I don't think it's a smile for real.

"If I'm not ready for Allison, she'll just skip me and go to Wendy's house," I plead. I know Allison likes Wendy better than me because at her birthday party last week, when her mom took us to McDonalds for the first time ever, Allison picked Wendy to sit next to her in the very back of the station wagon. Both ways. And Allison knows I love to sit back there, looking out the back window.

Dad stands up. He is tall, and I see his unsmiling face and cold brown eyes. Sometimes, like at Christmas or on vacation on the beach, Dad's eyes are a warm honey brown that I can almost melt into. But now they are like the hard, dark brown stones we pick up in Lake Michigan. His tan windbreaker is zipped tightly against the October wind. He doesn't answer me. I jab at dried-up oak leaves with my blue Keds, and then lean over and pick at the rubber toe caps. I am crying.

"Just stand by," Dad says. I think Dad learned stand by when he was in the Navy. He likes it because it means we can't leave until he is done, and with Car Cleaning he never, ever wants to be done, it seems.

"I gotta go Dad. Allison's coming soon and I gotta make my costume. It's Halloween, ya know." I push my brown bangs off my forehead with my sweaty hands, and I scrunch my forehead and rub my red eyes. "Not yet," Dad says. He doesn't see that I am crying because he is still sweeping dirt. Little, tiny pieces of dirt.

I do it. I leave Dad and run to the front door, pushing it open, and run through the small dining room to the kitchen where Mom is sliding foil rectangles of TV dinners in the oven.

"He won't let me go, Mom," I am crying. "Allison's gonna come and he won't let me leave him." I look at Mom; I never know if she will side with me, so my hands are really sweaty and my heart is pounding fast, and I wonder if I will be stuck back outside with Dad. Forget being best friends with Allison. Mom looks at me, and for one second I think I have lost. But she sets aside the potholders and unties her apron.

"Bruce," she yells, as she walks out the front door.

I am ready for Allison, even if I am still eating my Swanson's TV dinner when she comes. I have covered my red, swollen eyes with charcoal so she doesn't know I was crying.

Dad likes the candy bars with nuts.

Every Halloween night, we spread all our candy on the living room floor. In his green chair that leans back, Dad is reading his red magazine that says Time on the front.

Robbie and I pick out the candy bars he will like the best. The very best.

Dad puts down the magazine, and a man with blue eyes who looks really nice stares from its cover. I wonder if Dad could ever look like him.

"Just jump in and swim around and do what they tell you to do," Allison tells me every Saturday morning when we walk from my house, past Greeley School and six more blocks to New Trier, which is a big, huge high school that looks like a castle and is scary. But I don't like that I am supposed to dive in the pool all the time. I hate diving because I want my feet to go in before my head. "It's so cold," I say to Allison.

Allison and I walk through a side door, and ahead of us we see the big heavy gate that closes off the hallway, and we walk right to the open doorway, where a teenager stands in front of a big closet with shelves and lots of black bathing suits and white towels. "Here," I say to the boy, and hand him a yellow card, and he punches a hole in it and hands it back to me. "I'm eight," I say, and he reaches to a shelf and hands me a suit.

Allison and I giggle when we put on our suits in the locker room, because they are always too long. But that is the end of the fun part, because after that we walk through a little room with cold water up to our ankles, and then we shiver on the benches by the pool until our teacher gets us.

Every week when I get home, Dad asks "Did you pass?"

"Almost," I say one Saturday. "I can't dive yet."

"Next week you'll dive," Dad says. Then he goes outside.

I think Dad uses up most of his words with men during the week. Dad sells forklifts, which are little trucks, and Mom says he talks to men all day long and he is very, very tired after that. And that is why he doesn't use any words at dinner.

Besides swimming, there are other lessons in Winnetka. The moms send us off to swim lessons, dance lessons, sailing lessons and tennis lessons and I hate them all because I just want to be Me. All week long we have to be in stupid school, wearing a dumb dress and doing the stuff teachers tell you to do. Like we hardly ever get time to just read a book.

> "I just hated the whole thing. But you and Mom wouldn't listen to me and made me go, anyway," Beaver to Ward. "Now look, Beaver. Do you think for one moment that I'd make you do anything that would make you unhappy?" "Well, Beaver, I'm afraid we're going to have to make you do other things you don't like. I don't expect you to understand that."
>
> "Beaver's Dance," season 4, episode 21.

When I am reading, everything is good.

Saturday nights are not good. Mom puts on a suit like

Jackie Kennedy wears on the cover of Life magazine, and Dad wears a white shirt that comes in cardboard from the man that delivers them, and a boring suit, and they go Out. I like that we have a babysitter, and I like that we eat in the kitchen, and I like to play stop and go with Robbie in the dining room, using the silver cigarette box and shutting the lid when you stop. It smells good when you open it, like the smell when you go into Gram's house. We take the cigarettes out and breathe in the tobacco-ey smell. But I don't like going to bed on Saturday night.

There is a big empty hole in me when I lie in my bed, and I don't even feel like sneaking and reading with a flashlight. I think I have a hole because Dad never talks to me on Saturday except for words I don't like.

I don't tell him I am scared when he reads out loud to me and Robbie from his Wizard of Oz book before bed, during the week. I need Dad to love me, because Dad goes to work every day, all day, and makes the money Mom spends. There has to be a dad in every house, so if I please him, he will stay and do the job he is supposed to do.

This is my life. I know I must never, ever not do what Dad says, and I have to try as hard as I can to be good. Really, really good.

> "When a person's made a mistake or done something wrong, that's when they need understanding the most."
>
> Ward to Beaver, "The Lost Watch," season 2, episode 5.

I continue to yearn for Ward, even now. I cannot get enough of watching Hugh Beaumont bending over to regard Beaver's childhood concern with looks ranging from questioning, irritation, hidden laughter, and, ultimately, compassion and understanding.

I am four when I discover that a little tiny hope is bubbling up within me. It is on a cold winter Sunday morning that I make a startling discovery. On Sundays we don't have to do chores, and Dad uses more words, so the hole in my heart starts to go away.

Shredded Wheat and Grape-Nuts are the choice every Sunday. Mom leaves early to sing in the church choir, and since no one pays attention to the time, we tumble into the Volkswagen Bug shortly before nine, with little time to make it to the church service, zipping down Green Bay Road to church in the north end of Evanston. It is a massive brick structure where Dad grew up attending Sunday school. It feels strange, leaving Winnetka to go to church, and the alien, scary feeling of the big, dark building is only made worse by the fact I do not know my fellow Sunday-school classmates from school.

I am late, every week, and slip into a low chair, uncomfortable in my best dress and patent leather shoes and do my best to remain silent and unnoticed for the hour. I remember only friendly adults—usually a dad—talking about a baby floating down a basket in a river, or Jesus being nice to mean people. Then I leave.

Slipping on washed-out corduroy overalls and a T-shirt at home is akin, to me, to curling back up in my mother's womb. I am comfy; I have met some sort of confusing expectation and I have no worries for the rest of the day.

Mom is on her way home, and for now Dad is blissfully unaware of what I am doing. I run in stockinged feet the length of the living room, and dining room. Just as I collapse into a relaxed heap on the floor, rays of sun streak through the bay window and, I decide, I am OK. I will be OK. No one needs to tell me I am OK, because I just am.

It is my first discovery that God keeps the anxiety at bay.

CHAPTER TWO
"Art the Mailman"

Art the Mailman can drink a whole glass of water all at once.

I watch him, in our small rectangle of a kitchen, as the water slips past the flying monkeys on our Wizard of Oz jelly jar glass and through his lips as his bushy gray mustache twitches. He is very, very thirsty because it is humid, Mom says, and he walks a lot.

"We have orangeade," says Mom as she opens the screen door and asks him in. Art the Mailman walks all the way up to peoples' front doors and drops the mail through a slot in the door or puts it in a fancy box hanging outside. We have a very long walk because our house faces sideways. It's really not supposed to be a house but the house built next door a long time ago is so fancy that the guy who designed it got to build a little house to live in so he could watch all the work. Then he added stuff onto this one so it is a real house, and sold it. But it is crazy sideways.

Art hands Mom some letters and lowers his big leather bag to our black and white linoleum kitchen floor, right on the spot where Robbie has worn it from banging his chair down. "Just water is fine," he says, and sits in my chair at the round table.

Art the Mailman smiles, even when he is drinking water. His eyes get all wrinkly and I see a whole bunch of lines on his face. Watching him is not as fun as watching Robbie drinking strawberry milk, which makes the Cowardly Lion on the glass go from pink to clear, but still, it is very, very fun to have a mailman in my kitchen, and in my chair. He wears shorts with a blue stripe and has big legs with lots of hair, and a blue tie and a hat like Uncle Tom wore in the Army. When he takes his hat off, I can see the inside part is all dark; Art the Mailman tells me it is where he sweats.

"Do ya gotta write down notes when you get home?" I ask him. I am not shy around Art because he likes me. I don't know if Dad likes me so I don't ask him questions too much. Dad writes down lots of stuff in a black book he takes from a secret pocket right when he comes in the house at night. I figure men hafta do this at night.

"Notes," is what Dad says when I ask him, in high school.

I want a dad who walks in the door and smiles, like TV dads, so I know he wants to see me. As an adult, I realize what those notes were. Dad was so driven to succeed in sales that he painstakingly wrote minute details of his customers every evening. His commutes home along the Eden's Expressway, and later Columbia Avenue in Battle Creek, and I-90 back again in Chicago, centered on what he could do to achieve the next sale.

When I am seven, however, I am longing for the *Leave it To Beaver* dad. Every time Ward gets mad about something Beaver does, he decides Beaver needs explanations and understanding. Acting, I rationalize now when I watch Ward's expressions go from anger to frustration to awareness, and even disguised laughter. In the end, he understands and, bending down to look Beaver in the eye, assures him of his love.

Oh, how I wanted Ward.

"Well, I have to remember who wants corn, in the summers," Art says in answer to my question, "But I just remember in my head. Just fed the Greenblatt's cat," he adds as he puts his glass down. "They get home Saturday. I watered their plants but you might want to do it again tonight." He addresses this to Mom and I hope I remember which glass to pick for dinner, the lion glass, even though I like the Dorothy glass a lot better.

Art knows when everyone on my block is on vacation. He will feed cats, but not dogs, so we hafta take our dog Chessie to a kennel. And he gives away his corn, Mom says, because he is a very, very nice man.

I guess growing the corn isn't Art the Mailman's work, just the mail, because I think men always have to make lotsa money when they work. That's what all the dads in Winnetka do. A lotta dads I never see, like Joan's dad and Lisa's dad, because they travel, Mom says. I wonder if they are happy at night, or just write down all kinds of notes.

"How'd it go this morning?" Art asks me and Allison every day at the corner, when we walk back to school after lunch. He is always at the big mailbox; we watch him open it with a key and take all the mail out.

"I hate math," I tell Art.

Numbers are jumbly. They are dumb. Numbers feel cold, and they never change. Like you can go in the library, and every book is different, but numbers are all the same. No matter what I do, numbers don't change. I like words because they can make you happy or sad and change every time you turn a page. But I hate math.

It is Go to School night, in second grade, and I am supposed to show Mom how to use the number line—big black numbers pasted on the pink linoleum squares of our classroom.

"Just hop two more." Mom says. "You know which two."

But I don't know which two. My hands are sweaty, and I want to get off of this stupid number line in my dumb classroom and show Mom my SRA reading box instead. I am in the lowest group, orange, and I still have my yellow first-grade math workbook to finish. It is Mrs. Kramer's dumb idea that we hop on squares to add numbers.

My scruffy saddle-shoed feet remain glued to the number two square because I cannot multiply and add stupid numbers in my head, which Mrs. Kramer has called out to me, while people watch. Especially I can't think with moms watching me. And some dads.

Dad isn't here so he doesn't know I am dumb at math. I can add, kinda, when Dad tells us what our duties are worth.

"Five cents until you're eight," Dad says when I trade sweeping the front walk with Robbie for emptying the waste baskets. A buncha times a year we sit at the kitchen table with Dad to pick our duties, then he decides how much money we get for allowance.

"Robbie got ten cents." I want to be mad but I can't because Dad doesn't know what mad is and I just think about how dumb numbers are and how a nickel is much fatter than a dime, anyway. And I still don't believe Betsy that she says she can take a buncha dimes and nickels from me and give me a dollar bill and it is fair.

I am hugely deficient in math at a time when elementary class sizes of up to thirty kids, and zero existence of testing to recognize special needs, prevented any identification of this deficit, and I will stockpile grubby, plastic-spiral bound math workbooks with each successive grade so that I am woefully behind when we move from Winnetka when I am ten.

This will lead to hiding "Beany Malone" fiction inside my eight-grade algebra book, while elderly Mrs. Domain stands in her crepe-soled orthopedic shoes and teaches those who pay attention. High school geometry's formulas petrify me so badly, I reach the low of cheating to pass with D's, and it is not until I have to assist in entry-level high school math classes, as a para educator, in my 50s, that I face my fears.

"We always thought the teachers were helping you," Mom explains years later. In fairness, the progressiveness of Winnetka Public Schools meant math was often taught by the bigger-than-life Dr. Lola May, a tall, quick-speaking woman who rushes into our classrooms and flies about the chalk board. Report cards are not issued, simply progress reports. Homework does not exist.

The math education for most at Greeley School, I assume, worked well under the district-wide leadership of the late Dr. May. New Trier Township High School, which most of my elementary classmates attend, is a breeding ground for academic success. (I will not follow my friends to this high school).

Greeley is where I go to school until halfway through fifth grade. I start when I am three, and it is one block away from my house. I love a whole lot about Greeley because Mrs. Harriman, the kindergarten teacher is just like Gram, and there is a big art room that is messy, and a playground where we go all the time on weekends and a basement where Mr. Marinelli the Janitor has his very own bathroom and we get to go for air raid drills which means No Work.

Sometimes, after lunch, Chessie follows me to school. At the corner with the mailbox, Art tells me not to worry.

"He'll go home with me," Art says, and smiles real big as he stands up after bending over from taking the mail out of the big blue box. Art smiles just like Mr. Ned, on Bozo's Circus, which I try to watch after lunch if there is time. "Did you pick up your room this morning?" Mom asks,``Did you sweep the walk?" Both Mr. Ned and Art the Mailman make me feel like life is happy, and do not make me feel scary inside, like Dad does when he asks me questions. If I am crying when Chessie follows me to school, which I sometimes do because I am scared that Miss Murray, the principal, will yell at me, Art smiles the kinda smile I want Dad to do when I mess up.

But he doesn't. Dad scary is so bad, that the night he brings home the new Red Fuzzy for me, I cry real big inside me because it means I have done something right so he loves me. But not outside, not with tears. I cry inside because I am happy, but also confused about what I have done that is right. It makes me feel sad for Dad, and makes me cry.

I discover my loss of Red Fuzzy at seven years old, when we arrive home from a train trip to Denver and the suitcases are unpacked. I have left—abandoned—a six-inch long red furry strip with glued-on plastic eyes and an underside of stiffer material which made the furry strip gyrate when you stroked it, in my bunk in the sleeper car. A second-grade birthday party gift, my Red Fuzzy is clutched tightly in my right hand, every night, as I sleep.

Dad is a huge train fanatic and we take these overnight train trips several times in my childhood. When I tell him of my loss—it is a train story so I know he will care—he tells me, in a very caring moment, that my little "stuffed animal" will be happy "riding back and forth on the train." It is a Saturday evening, and he is cooking hamburgers on a small charcoal grill on our walkway, gazing west and pretending he owns a house that affords a good view of the sunset. "Red Fuzzy is in a great place."

This is not an era when a mom would contact a service industry to try to track down a small child's token, particularly one that undoubtedly is lost amidst a train car load of dirty sheets. At best, my toy is noticed in shreds in a commercial laundry machine.

Sometime later—was it two weeks, or several months or maybe even years? If it were possible, I'd track down Dad's business itinerary from 1963 and find out when he traveled to New Orleans on business. Dad comes home with one of the two gifts I remember his bringing me while traveling for work.

"Red Fuzzy." Dad, so tall and dark looking in his black suit and loosened tie, hands me a brown bag with script writing on it. He has taken it from his suitcase. I see a questioning look in his eyes, a look I have never seen before, and I want to cry. But I don't know why.

"It is Red Fuzzy," I say intuitively as I take the gift out. I clutch a block of wood with red yarn glued to it to resemble an animal of sorts. Black yarn makes up the head, and like my treasured toy, there are plastic eyes. A white ribbon is tied around the "neck" with New Orleans written in fancy script.

I barely register any disappointment over the stiff, almost scary-looking talisman because the need to give Dad the necessary approval is so much greater. "It's Red Fuzzy," I cry happily, and cradle it as best I can. "Thank you."

I keep Dad's version of my Red Fuzzy for so very long—how I wish I still had it—though never sleeping with this wooden block with yarn, and never feeling it is a replacement. At first I keep it because I must. Deep down, I know he cares. In between writing notes in his black book while waiting for a train, or plane, in New Orleans, Dad's eye catches a glimpse of red in a gift shop, remembers my lost Red Fuzzy, and buys me a replacement.

A little piece of him is not scared to love me.

Before I start kindergarten, I think that Art the Mailman is the Art who talks to the kids on TV and makes them say funny stuff like "I'm gonna be you when I grow up." The little kids sit in wire chairs on a stage and Art, who is old and smiles a lot, asks questions and laughs at what they say. I really want to be one of the kids that Art on TV talks to because I think he likes them a lot. A whole lot. I think it is a better job than selling forklifts like Dad does. Maybe Dad would smile a lot if he talked to little kids all day instead of boring men who want to buy forklift trucks.

The day after I see "House Party" on TV, when I see Art the Mailman at our front door I wonder how he gets from our street to the place where they interview the kids on the little wire chairs. But he smiles like the Art on TV so I guess he must drive there quickly and change into a suit like Dad wears.

Sometimes I walk with Art the Mailman, on Saturdays, from the big blue box at the corner to all the houses on our street. We have a very wide sidewalk, so I can walk right next to him. While he takes the mail to the front door, I trace the name in the sidewalk which is Paul Reschke, 1921. That is the man who made the sidewalk, Art tells me.

"Do you have kids at home?" I ask Art the Mailman. "I have lots of nieces and nephews," he says. I bet Art uses lots of words when he is at home but I don't know. Maybe there is no one to talk to at his house. I don't ask him, because all I want to know is that Art the Mailman smiles all the time.

"Your dad," my cousin tells me recently, "used to make me feel so safe. I mean, at family parties, he would just stand there, quietly, looking down at me. I always felt like if something bad happened, he would be right there."

I take comfort in my cousin's words. But isn't a dad meant for something more than just being around when something bad happens?

A psychologist will tell me, during a counseling session in my late 20s, that as a child I am trying so hard to please my dad to earn his love, I try to have no needs when he is around. "You didn't even think you could act like a girl," he says. "You had to be of the same value as your brother."

"They're lost," I say to Mom every morning after breakfast when I'm told to put on my school shoes, scuffed brown oxfords that are stiff and slippery with my tights or socks and no good for playing on the jungle gym. "Guess I'll just hafta wear sneakers." I shrug my shoulders.

School shoes—stiff brown oxfords and saddle shoes—and dresses and skirts that hindered playground time—plague me through kindergarten and another eight years of school. The more I look and act like a boy, the easier it will be for Dad to love me.

I am saved from dresses for my first year of kindergarten. In 1959, just after Labor Day, I am a few weeks away from turning four, and I happily ride the tricycles, swing on the monkey bars and finger paint under the watchful eye of Mrs. Harriman. Mom successfully lobbies that a four-year-old little girl shouldn't have to wear a dress to school; that little kids, be they boys or girls, want to sprawl on the floor and hang from the monkey bars and not give a single thought as to whether their four-year-old legs are pressed together. So, in the class group photo in February, I sit happily on my chair, dressed in soft, well-worn corduroys and T-shirt, while around me the eleven other little girls are in dresses.

Mr. Kryda, the PE teacher, is always on the playground before school starts. "How strong are you today?" he asks the boys. "Can you run any faster than yesterday?" he asks me and my friends Sarah and Allison and Laura. Mr. Kryda is really, really big and once bounced Hughie's Super Ball all the way against the top of Greeley. Hughie tells everyone, and no one else can do it but Mr. Kryda. He wears a shirt every day like the one Dad wears for golf, and tennis shoes and tan pants. I don't think Mr. Kryda has black suits, like Dad, and white shirts with cardboard in the collars that are delivered by a man in a truck. Maybe if Dad didn't have to wear a black suit every day—and got to be on a playground instead of selling forklift trucks—he would use more words on Saturdays.

Mr. Marinelli at Greeley wears the same green pants and shirt every day, with Tony written in fancy letters on a patch on his shirt, but we have to call him Mr. Marinelli. Mr. Marinelli never gets mad when you do something wrong. He fixes the zipper on my jacket when it gets stuck, and while he is doing it the smoke from his pipe comes into my nose and he kind of grumbles but he just fixes it. I always have to go find him in the basement, and he is always there. Every day.

Once on a Friday evening while chasing down a kick ball, I find Mr. Marinelli's wallet in the bushes on the playground at Greeley. I run straight home with this treasure, not even sharing my find with Robbie. "I'll keep it until Monday," Mom says, "and you can take it to him." This is over-the-top excitement because now Mr. Marinelli will like me even more, and talk to me, and that will be one more man I am pleasing. If I please enough men, maybe I will find a way to please Dad.

I go to find Mr. Marinelli right away in the basement on Monday.

"Mr. Marinelli, I found your wallet," I say to his back. He is bent over in his green uniform, at his work bench, and behind him I see the little bathroom he gets to use, just for him, with a toilet in it and no sink, which means he doesn't have to use the big bathrooms upstairs. I wait for him to smile real big and say "thanks Emily," and maybe hug me. Then I can tell everyone in my class that Mr. Marinelli talked to me and likes me.

"Don't know how I lost this," Mr. Marinelli says real small, and I can hardly hear him and his pipe is way over on the side of his mouth. I wait. I want more. Plus I want to miss the Agenda part of class where Mrs. Kramer tells us what is on the board. But Mr. Marinelli picks up his tool and keeps working.

I go back to class.

In second grade, in the class picture, I sit on the library chair between Laura and Cindy, and not next to my friend Sarah because the photography man tells us where to sit. Allison is not in the picture because she has a different teacher. Laura is my good friend, too, but she is tall and has to stand in the back row with the boys. I am wearing a red and white checked shirt with a blue skirt and around my neck is my dog tag with my name on it. "I belong to B.W. Thayer, 335 Fairview Ave., Winnetka, 446-1737," it reads. We wear round dog tags on long chains around our neck because our older sisters do it, at Skokie Junior High. It is a fad, Mom says. I am smiling, my eyes downcast, and all eight of us girls in this row have our hands folded in our laps. I am leaning forward, as if I am ready to move on. Sarah sits tall and straight and looks at the camera; she has a half smile. Between Sarah and me is Nancy, biting her lip, and appearing to be waiting patiently for the annual ordeal to end.

Maybe Art the Mailman and Mr. Kryda the PE teacher and Mr. Marinelli the Janitor are really nice to me because they are supposed to, because of their jobs. But aren't dads supposed to be nice to you too? I know if I want Dad to love me, I just have to keep trying, very, very hard. I wonder, is a man like my dad—or Art the Mailman or Mr. Kryda or Mr. Marinelli—the one who will marry me after I go to college and get smart and am ready to have a house like we have on Fairview? If he is like Dad, will I always have to try very, very hard so he will always love me?

> "Hey Dad, what's community property?" Wally asks Ward. "Well, community property means that your mother owns half of everything I earn or own." "What a gyp," Wally responds. "No wonder women get married. Mom, you sure got it made."
>
> "Beaver's Dance," season 4, episode 21.

CHAPTER THREE

"Barbie, Prom Queen"

Baba lets me have Ken when we play Barbie Queen of the Prom.

"We can *trade*?" I look at my "will-do-anything-you-want grandpa" from my perch on our blue nubby couch. "For real?"

Baba's long, khaki-covered legs straddle our coffee table so he won't bump our playing board with its stacks of little cards. I extend my pajama-clad arm with my recent boyfriend card pick to Baba. He accepts the card with red-haired, sorta-smiling Poindexter with tiny little eyes, and quizzical eyebrows and hands me his card with broadly-grinning Ken. A blob of white between his open lips means he has perfect teeth. And, his eyes are smiling.

No *way* Barbie wants to go to the prom with anyone but Ken. Everyone knows that.

"You got the bad one," I say. "Is that OK? I mean, I never get the Pep Club *and* Ken, too."

Baba's smile is so big I can see his gold teeth. He lifts a flannel-shirt-covered arm to rub his brow with two fingers, as if pondering the answer to a very important question. I see his big gold ring with a "T" on it on his finger.

"You can have him," Baba says.

He makes me toasted cheese when he babysits me and plays every game I want. Mom is at Junior League where she goes a lot so it is a very good day to be home sick from school because he is fun. I will not be very impressed with Mom's volunteer work. But then I learn that she pumped breast milk, while nursing all three of us, placed it in our tiny freezer, and donated it weekly to the Evanston Hospital Infant Welfare League for nine months after each of her pregnancies.

"Your turn," I hand Baba the two plastic dice and he shakes them gently and tosses them on the shiny, polished walnut coffee table. We have moved the silver cigarette box —with its fancy, scrolly letter T on top—and the glass ashtrays to the side. "You take my turn," he says. "I'm going to land on the square you want, so, you take it."

I eagerly move my token three spaces and nab the poodle-walking job, which earns me $2.50 toward my goal of buying the Enchanted Evening prom dress. To become queen and win the game, you have to buy a dress, have a steady boyfriend (a status earned by the shake of the dice allowing me to move my token through the "make a date" section, and then "go steady" section), and become a school club president. In the "make a date" section you have to pay some of your money, sometimes, if you go to the movies or a football game. But once you are going steady, your boyfriend pays for everything.

Earning money squares are good, too, because the best dress costs $65. You also collect an allowance from your dad. But you have to go backwards on the board if you land on a square sending you home because your hairstyle falls, or your hem falls out of your dress.

This game is marketed by Mattel in 1960 as "a fun game with real-life appeal for all girls." It is our parents' generation that is masterminding these games for their daughters, teaching them that looking the right way and being able to buy the right clothes earns you the ultimate goal, a steady boyfriend. The game clearly reflected popular values of the time.

I think Baba is scared of Dad.

"OK Bruce," he says, not smiling, when we go places together like restaurants. He is tall, and thin, and around me and Betsy and Robbie his body is like Gumby on TV—bending, reaching, and lifting to help us do anything we want. He once sat on the bathroom toilet for two hours, Mom says, holding my squirmy, toddler sister while she played in the sink. But around Dad he is like all the sheriffs on the Cowboy and Indian shows, kinda big and deep-down scared of the bad men.

A week later, Mom interrupts our Clutch Cargo watching to say we have to change from oh-so-comfortable play clothes back into school clothes because we are meeting Dad at a restaurant.

"Why?" Robbie says. He has all of the markers around him and is designing and drawing a multi-colored house on Mom's typing paper. I am waiting for him to add the people. Buildings are boring. I am on my stomach, making a house with the play tiles.

"We'll have fun," Mom says. But I am scared of restaurants with Dad unless we are on vacation. I hafta share a meal with Robbie, and never, ever get to have a fancy drink, even if the waitress asks me if I want one. Only milk. Restaurants where I hafta wear a dress are where Mom and Dad go on Saturday nights, and leave us with Vicki the babysitter and I go to bed that night with a big, empty hole in me. Good restaurants are Mary's Cupboard, when Dad is gone, and Betsy orders a black cow, and we get french fries and wear play clothes and the trains go by.

But I am anchored happily that evening, in a curved booth with red leather seats, between Baba and Mom, clutching a brand-new plastic doll. Words buzz above me, and today my siblings can't recall the evening and why we so unexpectedly met my grandparents on a weeknight. But that evening I am only intent on putting my doll to sleep on a sliver of space between me and Mom, under my bright white cloth napkin. I want no space between me and Baba, who gives me this doll with her painted smile, stiff curly black hair and tartan quilt and a little red jacket when we see him and Gramma in this restaurant. I nestle my hand around my doll, keeping in touch with things that are real to my six-year-old mind, and the red leather booth feels cool to my legs, even through my black tights, so I put my feet underneath my butt, and the stiff rounded edge of my brown leather school shoes cut into me.

We are enveloped by the dimness of this restaurant and I think I am not supposed to be here. I will have to hear Robbie get mad because he must give half of his dinner to me, but I don't mind because I know no one can hurt me. Baba is here, and I don't have to do anything to make Baba love me except be Me.

I can recall so little conversation between Dad and Baba during my childhood.

Were they scared?

This rejection of demonstrating their love is a genetic trait, I think, dangerously magnified on the Thayer side of my family with their profoundly undiluted New England-DAR-Mayflower Society descendant gene pool. Blessedly, Betsy, Rob and I—my paternal grandparents' only grandchildren—will all marry and have children with richly culturally and genetically-diversified partners.

My grandfather and father cannot easily say I love you. But Dad, like Baba, becomes a good grandpa for his eight grandchildren. And happily, my husband, brother and brother-in-law openly demonstrate their love.

> "You know that your mother and I love you very much, don't you?" Ward to Beaver. "And you know that anything we do is for your own good. Look son, when you think about this, you'll know I'm right. I'm sorry you feel this way."
>
> "Beaver's Big Contest," season 4, episode 6.

I am also scared of Gramma, though when I am alone with her, she will show me, through her limpid brown eyes and patience in reading all my made-up stories, that she has a very deep love for my siblings and me. She is a highly repressed woman, a victim of the times, and from being raised from age four on solely by her mother, a woman with deep Vermont New England roots and a spare, disciplinary attitude.

Perhaps had my great-grandfather Henry Harrison lived past age 32, Gramma's Chicago childhood may have been more lighthearted; old letters recount how he teased his older, highly pious brother when they were kids. My great -grandfather was good with people, these letters recount, and he was invited, as a young owner of a small downtown Chicago store, to go into business with Marshall Field. Following in the footsteps of his older brother (their father having died when the boys were toddlers), he attended seminary instead and launched a Christian weekly newspaper.

He was killed one evening as he stepped off a commuter train in the outlying suburb of LaGrange, their home, taking his customary shortcut across a set of tracks where an unscheduled oncoming train hit him, killing him instantly.

Constance, four, and her sister Faith, five, (names undoubtedly chosen to reflect religious values of their parents) would spend summers among aunts and uncles and grandparents in a big white farmhouse on Greenbush Road in Charlotte, Vermont, indoctrinating them with traditional New England values. Her mother moved them to Vermont for a year, and they walked down dusty Greenbush Road with their cousins to attend a small schoolhouse and faithfully went to the Congregational Church in a horse-pulled wagon every Sunday. But my great-grandmother was needed back in Chicago to help manage the finances of the Advance Publishing Company, a small company on Madison Street owned by her late husband and his partner.

For many years she is able to keep her LaGrange home, and could even afford the $50 tuition and $200 room and board and send her daughters to live on the campus of

Northwestern University in 1911. But on a chilly May day in 1912, the business manager of this small publishing company wrote a note saying he had mismanaged funds, and leaving the office in Chicago's downtown loop, plunged himself into the frigid waters of Lake Michigan. There was little money left, and my great-grandmother sold her home in LaGrange and rented a small house in Evanston, where her daughters could live at home and finish college. Eventually she would have to move in and share the home of her oldest daughter and her husband and children.

Three years before she was to graduate from Northwestern, on a warm Sunday evening in June, Baba arrives in his new "machine" at my grandmother's house and asked her to go for a ride. "Wonderful time," she wrote in a flourishing script in her diary, a crumbling brown artifact. They had dated since November and she was thrilled to have the attention from this serious young man who gave her a photo of himself in a track uniform with an N U emblazoned on it. She writes that he "runs after me," and they write many letters, devoid of emotion, to each other while he serves in the Army during World War I, after their graduation in 1915.

While their letters said little of their love, she was penning in her diary that she longed for when he would return.

They married a year after he returned, in 1919. There are no photos, unlike the wedding of my mother's mother, who married the same year after her husband returned from the same war and dressed in a white dress and boasted a wedding party of four. The photo of my Grandmother Noyes with her splayed wedding dress train sat in a silver frame on her dressing table during my childhood.

When did the discord with my paternal grandparents begin?

When did Connie begin to resent her older sister, Faith, who will have a daughter in 1918 and a son in 1920? Faith's son Harry is so much like an older brother to my dad—born in 1922—that I will think he is my uncle.

What made my grandmother carry a heavy rock of troubled emotions within her?

When did the silence enter my grandparents' household on Harrison Street and the like-mosquitos-buzzing-around-a picnic nitpicking begin?

"Mother, I have terrible news," I can imagine my grandmother might have said after one of the several times she learned she had miscarried. I see her sitting in the front hall of their corner, gray stucco home on Harrison Street in Evanston, where the black telephone sits on an antique end table. She still has hair down to her waist, and it is anchored on top of her head with pins. She is dressed nicely; women of that generation, in Evanston, often spent afternoons calling on each other. "I have miscarried my baby."

My siblings and I only know, from quietly spoken words from my mother, that Gramma suffered multiple miscarriages and was only able to have one child. Mom tells us she wanted more children, and that she found it difficult to raise an only child.

Did my great-grandmother Harrison, whom I know only from photographs and diary entries, rush over to comfort the younger of her two daughters? Or was my grandmother left to cry to herself softly in her bedroom, washing her face and straightening her hair before my grandfather returned home from work, and stoically telling him they had lost a baby.

I will miscarry, early in the stages of my third pregnancy, on my 39th birthday. I will leave the doctor's office, advised to let the fetus pass naturally, and with an urgent feeling that if I grocery shop, all will be fine. My young daughters are at a neighbor's, and when I have put my groceries in the car, I step up to a payphone and call my husband at work.

Tim's empathy and love pushes me through the weekend and subsequent days, yet two months later I am unable to be genuinely happy for a close friend who is through the first trimester of her third pregnancy. The birth of our third child, 15 months later, erases any sense of loss. I am so very fortunate. How would I feel now if I'd had no support?

Dad tells us his childhood is a happy one, and truly, I believe his mom and dad poured all their love into their son—this brown-eyed, dark-haired boy who grinned happily from his front row desk in third grade. He went to summer camp in Minnesota, ran track at Evanston Township High School, and spent many weeks in Traverse City, Michigan in the cottage owned by his Aunt Faith and Uncle Sam. Did my grandparents talk during those many weeks of a childless household?

When I am young, I often spend the night at their house. I sleep in Dad's old bedroom with its bedside lampshade of birch bark, and in the morning I crawl into Baba's twin bed. He tickles my feet and asks me if the bed bugs are biting. In the crisp new moments of the day, I sit in their breakfast nook and pour cream in a thin stream from the small, round opening of the cow pitcher onto my bowl of oatmeal, grasping the blue and white Delft pitcher by the cow's curlicue tail, and they sit quietly. I am the sole reason Gramma and Baba exist, at that moment. Baba stands up and deftly moves the hands of the cuckoo clock forward so I can see the intricately carved bird chirp eight times.

From the kitchen, Gramma brings warm, buttered slices of toast and I liberally sprinkle cinnamon and sugar from the cranberry-colored glass shaker on my slice. My breakfast is served on blue and white dishes, their pattern faded, and I imagine Dad sitting right here. After breakfast I dig holes in the alley with Baba's spade, near his one-car garage and later Gramma will lay out their big National Geographic book of maps and ask me where, in the world, I most want to go. She shows me Egypt and Africa and England and tells me I can travel wherever I want.

There are no questions Gramma and Baba will not answer. Why don't I ask them if Dad loves me?

It is confusing to know that your grandparents love you—that he will play the Barbie Queen of the Prom game with you, over and over, and she will read every single story you write in second grade and tell you that you can be a writer—yet they argue. Baba sits down next to me once, when I am 15, and looks me straight in the eye and says, "They're really lucky, you know, your mom and dad, because they like to do things together." I realize, now, how lonely he was; how he and my grandmother, somewhere in the midst of the Depression, World War II and living their lives, lost their ability to laugh and have fun together.

"He always talks too much," my grandmother says to me as my grandfather stands at the front door of their house. I am visiting for the day; I am eight and we are going to Fun Fair for the afternoon. This one-on-one time with my grandparents is to end soon. We are to move to Battle Creek. I sit in the quiet living room waiting for my grandfather to finish his conversation with the neighbor, and I have only the Grandfather clock with its creepy-looking face to divert my attention.

"He just talks a lot," Gramma says. "It's annoying."

I am aware there is a wedge between my grandparents, and I don't like it.

In a black and white photograph taken late in the evening on Friday, April 14, 1950, Dad is in his new Buick sedan, his right hand on the keys in the ignition. He looks into the camera with an eager look, smiling broadly and his eyebrows raised expectantly. Mom is seated next to him in a dress suit and hat and white gloves with eyelet cutouts, clutching a purse and smiling radiantly at the photographer. They are leaving their wedding reception at the Evanston Women's Club and headed to a hotel in Lake Forest. Mom looks happy and confident; Dad looks eager, ready to please. When I look at this picture, I feel like Dad wanted to be the best dad he could be—surely, they anticipated children to come. But I also sense that he does not know what lies ahead. He is 27; she is 24. I don't know if Dad is ready for this.

Why didn't Dad talk?

> "You know Beaver, I've never known a time when saying I am sorry didn't at least help a situation. I've made a lot of mistakes in my life but I've never made one that it didn't at least help to say I'm sorry," Ward tells a tearful Beaver, as he is comforted by June after confessing he spent his money on a toy for himself, and not for his brother Wally's birthday present.
>
> "Wally's Birthday," season 2, episode 1.

I think, now, as an adult, that this was living with anxiety as a child. Living with anxiety means I am not really sure I am supposed to be alive.

It meant then, and now—if I don't keep my anxiety in check—I must prove to myself, every day, to some great guru that I am worthy of existence.

Baba is my biggest fan. I just didn't realize it when I am a young adult. He will die at age 94, widowed for ten years, one week before my husband Tim and I get engaged. He will take his younger sister aside, when he is 90 years old, and tell her not to lecture me on my lifestyle and that even though I am her namesake, it is not her place to lecture his granddaughter.

It is a chilly May Saturday, in Evanston, and I am moving from a garage apartment to Chicago. My friends are helping me haul my belongings to a borrowed truck, and into the driveway comes my grandfather, navigating the turn slowly in his Buick. He is 90. Baba grins, and holds up a large bag. It is full of McDonald's hamburgers and french fries for me and my friends. This is my grandfather, who never asks for anything from me, but only gives his love and time.

He loved my Dad, I know now, just as my grandmother did.

Everyone loved everyone, for that matter.

It's just that no one said it.

CHAPTER FOUR

"Saved"

There is a place and time, in my childhood, where I am quite sure Dad loves me.

This would be easier to write had there been no time when I knew this.

But that would not be my story.

It is dark and deliciously scary when we walk up the wide, dirty red wooden steps to the car ferry in Milwaukee. "If he doesn't make it," I ask Mom, "will he come tomorrow?" I lift my right leg as high as I can to take the last, giant step onto the ferry, which will glide us silently through the summer night to a magical place. I am worried, frown lines creasing my four-year-old face, and my heart is pounding.

Betsy laughs, breaking the stillness of the inky black summer night. I look up to see the man in a double breasted blue blazer with rows of shiny brass buttons, extending his hand to help me over this last, big step.

"He always makes it, Emily," Betsy makes a quiet "duh?" sound without Mom hearing, but I don't care. This is my version of "A Magical Mystery Tour" (a journey we take twice every summer crossing the breadth of Lake Michigan to go to the Good Dad place, Watervale).

Dad will not be mad if he misses the ferry, I know. Mad is a scary thing; an emotion I never see in my father. When I am a child and young adult, Dad will never hit me, lie to me, intentionally embarrass me or outwardly hurt me. But I will be, from my very earliest memory, so anxious in his presence. The little boy inside my dad who was somehow hurt so badly will not let him show me he loves me for a very long time.

Except at Watervale.

Nothing can stop me from smiling big inside my tummy when Dad steps onto the ferry. I am mushy good inside, like taking the first bite of my very own not-to-share hot fudge sundae with whipped cream and knowing you have a whole buncha other bites before it's done. We will be together for the six hours it takes to cross the lake. There are lots of rules on boats and Dad knows exactly what they are.

And, I realize as the years go by, transitioning from selling fork lift trucks to Chicago area businessmen to a beach vacation without TV, phones or locks on the doors was easily done by my dad's getting on a boat.

We traverse from Milwaukee, Wisconsin to Ludington, Michigan twice every summer on the ferries and take week-end jaunts on the South American cruise lines to Mackinac Island on occasion. The weekend trips are a jumble of biting spring winds, and dresses in a fancy restaurant, and I don't have the happy car ferry feeling. In a black and white snapshot taken when I am five, Dad has gained permission from the captain for the three of us to stand outside the pilot's cabin. We line up in descending order under a black smokestack, and Betsy, the tallest at 10, is reaching for the hanging ship's bell, a smile across her face that says she is doing as Dad wants. Robbie boasts the captain's white hat with its gold crest and stands with chest puffed out, hands held rigidly at his side. I look lost, a dazed grimace on my face underneath windswept, too-short bangs and my arms hang awkwardly in my Sunday wool dress coat I hate. I have unbuttoned it to keep the velveteen collar away from my face.

I don't know, until I am well into my twenties, that Dad saves the ticket stubs from every boat trip we take and puts them in the corner of his mirror, until his next trip.

At Watervale I feel little anxiety around Dad, so this timeless place in a corner of northwest Michigan is one I return to whenever I can, as an adult. It is the caring, solid, Midwest people who own this pristine spot of land bordering two lakes that make it such an escape, I realize much later in life. With an uncanny foresightedness in 1900, a Chicago bachelor bought the acreage, with its abandoned lumber camp hotel and cottages, and welcomed his six siblings and their families to vacation. By the end of World War I, the resort was attracting vacationing families, and he eventually would pass the resort down to a niece who loved, cherished and protected the land from developers.

I was in utero when I was first taken to Watervale, and had we been able to live in this place where the grandmotherly owner treated Dad, and everyone else, with love and kindness, perhaps the wide-eyed, sparkly-eyed grin that Dad displays in his grammar school photos would have remained.

On the ferry Dad inserts a very long, thin, silver key into a door and we are in a secret bedroom—a stateroom—with a toilet, a sink and a window to the outside. We tug on handles on the wall and out pops a freshly made bed with crisp white sheets, and a thick brown wool blanket. Betsy and I lie head to toe in the single bed, and the next morning we hear a sharp rap on our stateroom door and a man announcing "Ludington."

"Are you five?" Dad asks me, looking up from signing the index-card sized registration at the glass-topped front desk in the Inn. It is mid-morning and we have just arrived, after breakfast in a Ludington restaurant and the one hundred-mile drive north. I peer up at him, smiling, because I know he is the Watervale Dad now and his eyes will be happy all week. "No," I giggle. "I'm four. And Robby's seven, I think."

"Betsy's nine," Robbie offers, as he hops on one leg while Dad completes the card with his long, slanty handwriting. "Can I go get the boat?"

I don't think it is odd that Dad doesn't know my age. This is the only time he asks such a question, and I am thrilled for the attention.

Because Robbie is a boy, he is allowed to row our boat all alone, along the shore, to our cottage. Dad drives our brown Buick down the dirt road and lifts the big tan leather-trimmed suitcase out of the trunk and into one of the three tiny bedrooms. It is only minutes before we are changed into bathing suits and encased in our faded pink life jackets and Dad is rowing us to the outlet, a wide stream of water connecting the smaller inland Herring Lake to Lake Michigan, where we will play for hours.

"Can I take this off?" Robbie plucks at the ties on the bulky life jacket, as soon as Dad starts rowing. He is bare chested like Dad and squirming next to Betsy perched on the small seat in the bow. I sit next to Mom in the back, a picnic in front of us and our dog Chessie behind us. The green metal boat with its wooden seats is heavy, a U.S. government World War II surplus row boat, and like the ferry, I feel safe in this confined space, with Dad's strong muscles tensing every time he strokes the oars backwards. "At the point," Dad says. "Where it's shallow." We are together and cannot go anywhere unless Dad leads us. Robbie has to follow the rules because you have to sit still in a boat or it will tip, Dad says, and even Robbie is scared of that.

How do I describe a place, where, in my mind, it is always summer, and Dad smiles, and there is no Scary Dad or car cleaning and the only thing you hafta do is brush your teeth, try the vegetables at dinner and wear the pink life jacket in the rowboat?

"We know Watervale," my classmate Brad writes in "Our Summer Plans" book in first grade at Greeley School. The construction paper booklets we all take home consist of twenty six purple-inked mimeographed sheets of paper, with crayon drawings, highlighting every classmates' anticipated summer plans. "There is a dock, and a boat and we swim, and swim," Brad writes.

It is a simple summer resort where families play on the beach, swim and take long walks and eat dinner nightly in the turn-of-the-century Inn where tanned college girls bring us plates of baked chicken and mashed potatoes, and ice cream sundaes.

By virtue of the owners' foresightedness and generosity, efforts from the Grand Traverse Regional Land Conservancy and individual contributions, Watervale's shoreline along both lakes remains virtually the same today as when the land was purchased over one hundred years ago.

We are a one beach-towel-family at Watervale. That's a Dad rule, but it's OK because I am in the sand and the water only—all the time—and there are so many sand castles Robbie and I must build along the outlet that we are very, very busy. I leave the water's edge to gobble a hot dog charred over the fire Dad builds, and drink sun-warmed lemonade; pee in the long beach grass, and to take my plastic bucket to where Dad and Betsy hand dig a channel to keep water flowing between the two lakes and play and scoop out sand.

At the linen-table-clothed dining room table in the inn, I am sun drenched and drowsy, little interested in the plain, simply cooked meat and potatoes meal, so Dad shares our plates and we are sometimes allowed a nickel afterwards to choose an Oh Henry! candy bar, Hershey Bar, Peppermint Patty or Tootsie Roll from within the glass display case in the lobby.

"They jump off the ferry, and the water is dark, and deep."

Dad speaks in a quiet, rumbly voice while he perches on the edge of the bed Betsy and I are sharing. His shadow looms large on the wall next to me. I shiver in fear (and from the after-effects of my sun-reddened shoulders). "They're scared, but there is Mrs. Horsey Feather in a row boat to take them home." Dad leans over us and nuzzles our foreheads with his "nearly a bedtime kiss but not really" show of affection. The Watervale Dad is here and I am sunburnt and even though the sand in the bed will scratch my burn, I am happy because Dad says you hafta get burned to get tan. He thinks suntan lotion is dumb but Mom is always trying to put it on us.

Mornings are best at Watervale because I wake up happy in my tummy knowing there is a whole day ahead. Dad and Robbie and I go to eat our breakfast at the Inn before the kitchen is even open, and we wait on the big chairs on the porch, listening to the waitresses getting ready. We eat mostly alone, before anyone else is up, and I think Dad likes me and Robbie best because we get up so early with him.

"It's magic here," my best Watervale friend, Sally, says. It is the next day, and we are lying on our bellies on the Lake Michigan beach, burying our hands deeply in the sun-drenched sand until we feel cool moist pockets of water. I only see Sally at Watervale. Dad is standing next to our beach fire, hotdog in one hand and an amber bottle of Stroh's beer in the other. His best buddy from high school, Sally's dad Dave, drinks a beer next to him and makes Dad laugh, something I can't do.

Watervale is even better when Sally and her mom and dad and Sue and Chuck come too. Why, I wonder now, did my father not have a friend like Dave at home?

"Take three shots," Dad says as he hands me golf-ball sized rocks from the shore. "Then it's Sally's turn." Dad reaches back with his muscled, tanned arm and tosses the brown bottle into the frothy waves of Lake Michigan. I toss my stones, trying to shatter the bottle. Bottles are frequently seen on the shoreline in the 1960s and a favorite activity is to see who can shatter the glass. The result is rounded, smooth, multi-colored beach glass we gather every summer and take home.

Later, on a walk, we dig out clay-like mud along the ground springs in the dunes and rub the goop on our cheeks in bold, brown stripes. "Indian war paint," Dad says, and helps us collect glass jars full to take home. The clay dries on our sunburnt faces and cakes off, and we smear more on to keep alive our game of Indians Hiding in the Dunes.

I want it to always be just me and Dad and Robbie and Betsy and Mom at Watervale—and Sally and her family—because we are full up with fun stuff to do, with just us. For many summers we must have our Bottle Cap War, boys against girls. It is one of our ingenious, conservation-minded dads who dreams up this activity, which amuses us for hours, until another resort family rents a motor boat one summer and offers water skiing for families who chip in for costs.

The Bottle Cap War has us six kids spending most of the week collecting discarded soda pop bottle caps from the beaches, the sidewalk running the length of the turn-of-the-century cottages, the woods behind the Inn, or from the two soda machines at the resort where the caps are popped off with a quick jerk on the embedded openers. Hours are then spent hiding our paper sack collections, buried according to a treasure map we make. The actual war between the two boys and four girls, that our Dads mention every evening will take place the last afternoon, never quite occurs. We all envision hurling fistfuls of bottle caps at each other on the beach, positioned behind the dunes, but in fact the bottle caps, once unearthed from their shallow hiding spots, are deposited by our dads next to the soda machines where they will be picked up by the man who refills the machines weekly with Dad's Root Beer, Squirt soda, Orange Crush and Grape Nehi soda. Our dads are not to blame for the peace treaty; somehow Betsy and Susan, the oldest of all six of us, become convinced by weeks' end that the war is "dumb."

All too soon, by the time she is 13, Betsy becomes so enamored with a summer camp in Minnesota that she will spend a year's worth of babysitting money to help pay for twelve weeks there, ending a true family trip to Watervale. It is the same time that Robbie grows bored with our beach afternoons and convinces Dad to let him water ski, a gas-guzzling activity our father disdains, and our family bond that I so cherished is gone.

> "I was just thinking about how much closer the family is up at the lake," Ward to June. "Wally, there's just one thing I'd like you to bear in mind. The family's one place you're always wanted. And don't you forget that."
>
> "Untogetherness," season 5, episode 39.

In a photo taken the summer of 1965, my parents sit on wooden chaise lounges with thickly padded cushions in front of our cottage. Dad is with a book and has a satisfied smile; Mom holds a cup of coffee and saucer in her hand, with a

Jackie Kennedy look in a white beach jacket, earrings and lipstick. Robbie perches, bare-chested, on the edge of Mom's chair, an eager glint in his eye hinting of joining the others on the ski boat down at the lake.

I kneel between the chairs, wearing cut-offs and a hand-me-down surfer shirt of Robbie's, a happy little-girl look on my face, and not nearly so eager to join the older kids at the motor boat. I know these families from years at Watervale, but I don't want to give up the Dad Time. I don't want to lose the Watervale Dad by leaving him alone. Will he be happy?

When I am in high school, Dad and I find our common ground again at Watervale. I am a tomboyish, self-conscious teen uncomfortable with my femininity, so we spend hours on the tennis court. I avoid the motor boats because I want these teenage boys I have known all my life to like me, and instead they ignore me.

Mom loves life beyond the row boat and beach picnics at Watervale, and embraces the 1960s cocktail scene, dragging Dad to cottage gatherings before dinner. In one of the most glamorous photos I have of my mother, she is sitting in our cottage, dressed for dinner in a simple knit dress, with pearl earrings, carefully applied lipstick and well-coiffed dark brown hair, the result of her beauty shop appointment the day before we left, and avoiding getting her hair wet all week. But what is most dazzling is her smile. I am eight; she is 39. I sit next to her in a simple cotton dress and smile shyly, my yet-to-be restrained buck teeth protruding and hands in my lap, looking at Dave holding his Polaroid Instamatic while Mom smiles as if the world is waiting for her.

Another photo, taken a year or two earlier, shows a group

of us eating lunch at a favorite restaurant near Watervale, something our mothers would have done with us if our fathers played golf. In this photo, I look at the camera awkwardly, almost glaring. I do not want to be in a restaurant, and my faded jeans and rumpled white Watervale sweatshirt with a green pine tree means I wanted only to be playing on the beach.

We, the Thayers, quickly become part of the Watervale social scene, and all too soon alone time with Dad vanishes. Mom loves the evening cocktails, and I follow Robbie to the often-painful card games of bloody knuckles with our friends. Robbie loves the group bonfires on the beach at night, where someone's dad brings a cooler of sodas and bags of marshmallows to toast in the licking orange flames.

I am insecure enough to feel scared when, after a day of playing with just Sally, we all gather at twilight on the Lake Michigan beach. All the older kids that Robbie has careened down the dunes with in old truck tire inner tubes all day are there. Someone's dad has just lit a large bonfire. He stands with a can of beer in his hand, joking with dad number two.

I want to sit by the fire with Sally and watch the dancing flames and hear the lapping waves. But Tom, Dave, Becky, Paul, Chuck, Andy and everyone wants to run and hide in the recesses of the dunes, our bare feet splaying the evening-chilled sand in all directions. We play Pom Pom Pull away, chasing each other and I try to stay close to Sally. Soon a couple of the boys twist the rules, tagging a girl and tumbling on the sand with her, gently inching towards the privacy of the dunes.

Once twilight has passed, and only stars illuminate the

beach, the dads call us back to the fire and open a cooler of grape Nehi's, Orange Crushes and Squirts. One night I run to the cooler to see only one Orange Crush left. Orange Crush is Robbie's and my favorite treat—a coveted one—so I grab it.

Robbie is still playing among the dunes. "I saved it for you." I hand my sweaty-faced brother the tall glass bottle filled with bright orange soda when he comes running up a few minutes later. "It's the last one. I didn't get any." I save it for him because I think I must; females must always put men first. Surely, he will share it with me, and maybe even try to include me with his friends.

"Thanks," he says, and he means it.

A mental health counselor will tell me, twenty-five years later, that I still can't grasp the bottle of my favorite soda—or anything else—if any man in my life will be displeased.

When I am very young, Watervale becomes a very scary place. It is evening, and Mom tells me a generous business-man from Detroit is distributing a stock load of toys from Kresge's, where he is a buyer. If I will walk all the way to the end of the Watervale sidewalk, where there is a cottage I have never been to, I can get a toy.

New toys are on your birthday and Christmas, so this out-of-nowhere offer to have a new toy, at four years old, is the hot-fudge-sundae feeling.

"Brad will be down there," Mom says. "You know Brad from kindergarten."

Dad is not going to go with me. The Dad routine at Watervale is swimming, beach, dinner and beach again to see the sun go down. Dad is not going to the other end of

Watervale, which will take ten whole minutes to walk to. Mom will go, but I do not want to go without Dad. I am not sure where my siblings are on this evening. It doesn't matter. I don't want to go without Dad because we are at Watervale.

The desire of a new toy is stronger than my fear of leaving the Watervale Dad, and I follow Mom down the sidewalk where children are lined up on the boat house to dangle a fishing line down fifteen feet where Mr. Mertins stands like Santa Claus, with cartons of toys. I see tow-headed Brad and call to him, but he is playing with friends he knows. I stand with pole in hand and call down my name and age to this very generous Mr. Mertins, and soon I'm hauling up a tissue-paper-wrapped toy on the hook.

I love the new doll, with its orange hair and green striped dress, and I want to turn and walk back down the long, long sidewalk to my cottage, before it gets dark, and find Dad.

"You have to thank Mr. Mertins," Mom says. I clutch the new doll. "No," I scream inside. Talking to a new person is not part of the deal. And I have to get back to Dad.

"Once you thank him, we can leave," Mom says.

I manage to choke out a thank you to the smiling man, once I have walked down the concrete steps where he is standing. But I have the hole inside, and I am mad at Mom because Watervale is where there is just good stuff.

No have-to's. Not while I have the Watervale Dad.

On our boat trip home from Michigan, we board the boat in Ludington at lunchtime, and soon after it sails out of the harbor Mom and I stand on the pink-linoleum-covered steps leading up to the dining room to wait for a table for lunch. Lunch in the car ferry dining room looks like lunch in a fancy restaurant, except no one worries. Sometimes the waves are high outside in the lake and I can't eat my turkey sandwich, but I try to because it has fancy toothpicks in it with curlicues, and potato chips. When the waiter brings the sandwich, it is on a blue and white china plate with a blue boat in the middle and writing underneath that says Pere Marquette.

If I don't eat it, Dad doesn't have to pay for it because the waiter writes seasick on the bill, but if I do, I get to order a Dixie cup of ice cream with chocolate sauce on top. It is very good, and then we get to run all over the boat while Mom takes a nap in the stateroom. If she is happy when she wakes up, she gives us a dime to get a Nestle Crunch out of the vending machine in the lounge. Then it is a very good day even though Watervale is all done.

Dad's ashes are buried in a small township cemetery just a short walk from Watervale, and a sprinkling of childhood friends who also loved the summer magic of Watervale, are returning now, for retirement. And now I finally want to play with them—to remember how Dad's sharpness softened, and his anxieties melted away as he walked the Lake Michigan shoreline with me.

CHAPTER FIVE
"WHY?"

Jim's milk-chocolate brown face stretches into a smile as I run up his front porch steps, and I watch the smile lines spread across his leathery face, and see his gold-capped tooth. He is happy to see me. Jim loves me like no one else, I think. There is no one else in the whole world who is so happy to see me.

"Miss Nancy," Jim says to Mom, and reaches out his shaky hand to enfold her's. He chuckles, a rumbling that starts deep in his chest with a laughter that takes almost forever to come busting out of his lips; it spills over me. I know I can do nothing wrong at Alice and Jim's house. Jim's smile is so big that I wonder if his face might break.

Alice stands behind him, eyes sparkling behind cat's eye glasses and reaches out to hug me. Jim's firmly planted his hands in the pockets of his gray pants with the little tag in the back that says Dickies, and keeps smiling.

Jim and Alice always come out on their front porch to say hi, even in winter, when we come to visit them in their small grey bungalow in northwest Evanston. I change after school to my play clothes and my faded red Keds with rubber toe caps and I am comfortable, inside my body and out, because I think Jim loves me more than any other man.

No one else in the whole world seems so happy to see me when I visit, except maybe Gram who hugs me with her cigarettey smell. It is easy for moms and grams to show how much they love you, but not dads or any other men. I guess it is another rule, except not for Jim. I also like to come to Alice and Jim's house because they have brown skin. They are colored and the only other colored people I know are Rosa, who lives in the upstairs of Alice and Jim's house and is at Gram and Gramp's house all day and makes cookies and stuff, and also the lady who cleans our house every Thursday. I only see Rosa and the cleaning lady in white uniforms, so it is fun to see colored people in real clothes.

When I am home there are too many things I can do wrong. And at Greeley, where I am in second grade, I don't think I ever do math right, which is why I am always in the Yellow Group, the lowest. My best friend Sarah's dad kinda yells when we do something wrong like spilling the milk, but that is because he wants us to be smart, he says. I don't know how getting mad at someone makes them smarter. Irritated, is what Sarah's dad says, not mad.

I just know that Jim will never, ever yell at me or even be mad at me.

On the porch, Jim is bent over, just a little, and I can see the little tight curls of grey hair on top of his head. They are very old, Alice and Jim. Alice's braids on top of her head are all grey. They are retired, Mom says, just like Baba and Gramp. Alice was very, very nice to Mom's grandmother and took care of her until she died, and Mom says she wants to visit Alice until she dies, too.

Dad never visits Alice and Jim because he is at work.

"Jim," I say first thing, "I can catch the overhand balls Dad throws to me now!" I talk quickly, kicking my Keds against the porch steps and making little pieces of gray paint fly into the bright sunshine. I want Jim to hear me before Robbie says I am not so good and that I only caught one ball last night and a bunch of other ones went out in the street. I look up and see Jim's smile spread even bigger, and I wonder if his face will just break open. Jim doesn't use very many words, just like Dad, but he laughs so much that I think he is the happiest person I know. Even happier than Art the mailman. And he is laughing, always laughing.

Jim grins and I get the excited feeling in my stomach as we go inside and he stoops down to pick up the Lorna Doone cookie tin from the bottom of the wire TV stand. Some feeling like sadness washes over me; a layer of dust coats the blue top of the cookie tin, and I think that no one else plays marbles with Jim except us. But then Jim bends over very slowly, taking a really long time to kneel on the floor, and finally he is there and spilling out the shiny round marbles, small and large, and Robbie and I herd them into a circle on the wooden floor.

I am not as good as Robbie at shooting marbles so Jim covers my hand with his, guiding me through the flicking motion. My big blue marble shimmers as it breaks into the circle of glossy round orbs, and marbles scatter down the narrow hallway to the kitchen, some into dark, cobwebby corners.

"I can't shoot it straight like you," I say, positioning a small tiger-striped glass orb before my thumb and first finger. "It goes crooked."

He smiles, pushes his black-rimmed glasses back up on his nose and grips my hand tighter. "Hold your wrist steady." His face is one huge smile as he helps me shoot the marble straight into the cluster of multi-colored orbs. "You can shoot straight," he says, chuckling and pleased with his success. "You sure can."

We never play outside at Alice and Jim's, so I don't know what their backyard is like. Once I asked Mom how come Alice and Jim live in a house if they are colored. When we take the L to Chicago we see where the colored people live, in tall houses next to the train tracks that have lots of families living in them. They are apartments, Mom says.

"How come Alice and Jim live in a house just for them and they don't have clothes hanging from a line on their porch?" I ask Mom on the twenty-minute drive from our house in Winnetka to Alice and Jim's house

"A lot of colored people live in houses," Mom says. "You're just seeing the apartments the colored people live in, on the way to Chicago." I know it is colored people living in those houses with the laundry because once a friend came with us and he said niggers live there. I asked at dinner what a nigger was, and both Mom and Dad got really mad and said never to say that word. Later Mom told me that nigger is a very mean word for coloreds.

In the book "Back to School with Betsy," which I read at Greeley last year, Betsy asks her mom for a "little colored baby" brother or sister. I ask Mom "'Did Betsy want a blue or a yellow baby?'" Mom said Betsy means a baby with dark skin, like colored people. In the book, Betsy's mother tells her that colored babies can only be adopted by colored mothers and fathers. When Mom says colored people, she says it real nice, but when Baba says "coloreds," he starts talking about how there are too many in Evanston, and he gets a sad look on his face.

It feels mixed up, to me. Gramp always says to Rosa that "We couldn't live without you," so why does Baba not want so many coloreds to live in Evanston?

We never see Alice and Jim's kitchen; we only look into it as we play marbles in the hallway floor. A faded color photo from 1960 freezes a moment in which two of my cousins are in the front yard outside Alice and Jim's home. Alice is handing flowers from her garden alongside the house to five-year-old Cate, and Jim is slightly stooped, as if answering a question of four-year-old Steph. They are bathed in sunlight and I imagine my cousins, visiting from Colorado, feel very loved at that moment.

After marbles, Alice brings out cookies like Rosa makes, not like the kind Mom buys at the A&P, and we sit on the couch, and she asks questions all about me. Alice remembers the answers, because she writes poems about me and my cousins at Christmas and gives them to Gramp. Alice writes that when I am five, after we play marbles at their house, "next piggy back was Emily's choice. Jim, being the horse, had no voice."

To 1227/
Emily and Robbie came to call/
Immediately up to Rosa's room they flew/
Not finding her/
Back downstairs they came/
Robbie instantly proposed a marble game
Next piggy-back/
was Emily's choice/
Jim, being the horse/
had no voice.

I think Alice and Jim did not have kids because Alice worked really hard to take care of my great-grandmother and Jim worked every day at the railroad. In all the poems Alice writes she says she has "deep respect and much gratitude" for Gram and Gramp. Mom says Alice has been writing the poems since 1935, when Mom was 10 and Uncle Tom was three. Broken arms from football, clandestine cigarettes in the garage attic and high school plays fill Alice's poems in the 1930s, always sprinkled with thanks to my grandparents.

Alice, I learn, is brought to Evanston when she is eight years old from Muscatine, Iowa by her parents. Her father owns a store, and why, in 1895, he uproots his family for the growing city of Evanston is not clear. Her parents were both born in Tennessee and somehow migrated, separately, to Muscatine where they marry on Wednesday, October 6, 1886.

I am told by an elderly woman recently that Alice had a

chance to go to college. I meet this friend of Alice's through the Baha'i Temple archivist, in Wilmette, Illinois. Alice was a long-time member of the Baha'i faith. "Alice told me she was ready to board a train in Chicago, for the university, but a friend rushed up to her at the last minute with some news, and she changed her mind."

We never spoke with Alice, or Jim, about their pasts.

"She went to free lectures in the evenings at Northwestern (University)," my elderly acquaintance tells me. "Afterwards she'd take students' graded papers out of the trash and take them home to read. She was always learning."

Jim Moor was born in Chicago in 1893. He married at 19 and lost his first wife when she died delivering a stillborn child. He married Alice in 1934, she was 47 years old and he, 41. Thirteen years later they purchased their Leon Place home for $2,200, assuming the $75 monthly mortgage. They rent the second story, a small, one-room-sloped-ceiling apartment, to Rosa.

A vivid watercolor painting of Alice, by my Great-Aunt Bey, has Alice with her eyes fixed into the distance, a red and white polka dot kerchief tied over her hair, a blue dress on and a large ring on her right hand. "Wasn't she a maid?" one of my daughters asks me when she is six. We live in Vermont, and my children will not know many people of color until we have a refugee family from Somalia live in our home for a few weeks.

"They were our friends," I say simply to my daughter. "Jim played with me, and he never, ever did anything but love me."

We live just four miles away from Alice and Jim until I am 10, and in that time they never come into our house.

I don't know if they are invited. Nor did I ever go into a restaurant or store, or anywhere in public, with either of them. Sometimes Alice and my mother grocery shop together, and always Alice insists on walking in the store separately so Mom will not get hostile stares.

I love Jim because I know he accepts me for exactly who I am.

Today, as I look at the so few photos we have of this elderly couple, I think Jim planted his hands firmly in his pockets because every fiber in his being prompted him to enfold us in a hug. But he couldn't.

In a black and white photo taken in the winter of 1960, Alice sits in the chair of a second-story bedroom at my grandparent's rambling three-story Evanston home. The backdrop is the flowered wallpaper and frilly white curtains I see every time I spend the night there. Alice is wearing a checked dress with an open neck and large buttons on the front. It is adorned with a gold butterfly pin, and she is wearing simple earrings, a gold watch and a bracelet. And a hat. I imagine she has just changed from her white uniform. Her hands are folded and she smiles but her eyes are downcast and portray sadness. Is she thinking, at 73 years old, that she will only sit in this room briefly, posing for a picture? Is she wondering why the house isn't hers, simply because of the color of her skin?

When I become an adolescent, I realize it is not OK to love black people as if they are your grandparents, if you are white. Our visits dwindle, once we leave Winnetka, to Thanksgiving only. A 1973 home movie shows Jim shaking hands with Rob, 20, and with me, 17, standing self-consciously off to the side. In my mind Dad is absent, but I think that perhaps he came with us and shook hands with Jim on the front porch.

This, sadly, is the last time I will see Alice and Jim. On a Thursday in August, 1975, while I am working at Watervale, Jim Moor signs a Declaration of Belief at the offices of the Baha'i Temple in Wilmette, becoming a member. Alice had been a member since 1932.

I like to think that, in their last two years, they shared their common faith, and that both took great pleasure in that. In April, 1977 Alice died in a nursing home at 86 years old and three months later Jim died in St. Francis Hospital in Evanston, at 80 years old.

I wish I could write that I knew, at the time, of their deaths and that Mom attended the funerals. My cousin did. Their obits are simple; they had no children. Jim lies in an unmarked grave in Rosehill Cemetery in Chicago, next to Alice, who has a simple headstone. I can find no living relatives or even close friends of Jim's. Someday I will put a stone there, but first I must find the people who loved him.

How could they give us such unconditional love?

Jim died before I could tell him what his friendship meant to me; before I could learn about him and what he had done with his life. Before I could tell him that I was his friend because he was the nicest man I ever knew. Jim gave me the love I could not ask my father for. I asked my father, later, and he gave it freely.

Does Jim know what a great gift he gave to me?

I loved him; and I have the memory of Jim's smile that nearly broke his face.

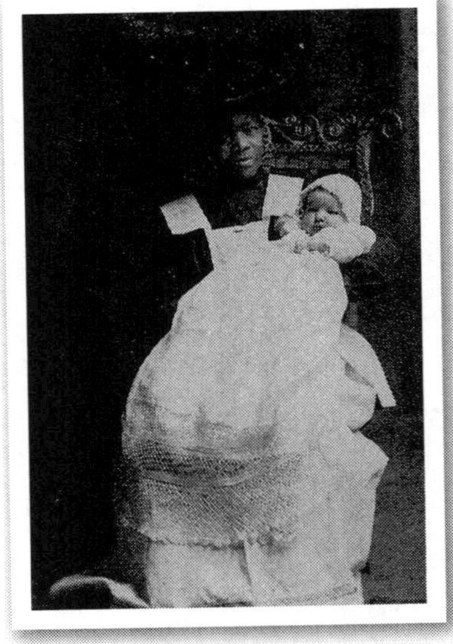

CHAPTER SIX

"Old Black Mary"

If Robbie lets me have the seat next to the window, I can play Mom being Mean and the ride goes quick.

"You *cannot* go," I whisper to the girl doll on my lap, while I wave the mom doll with the yellow hair in my right hand. "You have to clean the attic." The girl doll whimpers, and she is swooshed under my left thigh, quickly, before Robbie can laugh at me. It is just after lunch on a Sunday, in May, and we are driving, for a whole long hour, to the farm. It is a warm spring day, and we drive with the windows open. I feel happy because it is bright outside and the air coming in feels good and not sharp and cold like winter.

The place where you put your arm in Dad's car in the backseat is just long enough for three dollhouse furnitures, so I bring the bed, the toilet with a seat that lifts and the refrigerator. Dad only lets me have three furnitures anyway. "If we're in a car accident, they could fly up and hit you in the eye," he says. I can also bring three dolls.

I always choose the mom doll, with yellow hair, and two kid dolls. I make the mom doll be the dad too.

"You can't, can't, can't go to the birthday party," the mom doll says again. "You both have to be in the attic all day because you were bad!" As I whisper, I press my body against the car door and the arm rest because I want to be far away from Robbie so he won't laugh at me. He thinks my game is really dumb. The mom is mean to the girls because they are orphans who are adopted and don't know all the Rules.

We go to the Farm when it is kinda warm out, but not good enough for Mom and Dad to play golf, which is what today is. Dad put the top down on the way home from church, and said it was finally time to wear shorts, so right when we get home I run up to Betsy's room and push her desk chair over to the shelves high up in her closet, and dig through the summer clothes boxes. This is the best time of year because all the good stuff is ahead, and Dad is in a good mood.

"It's a farm day!" Great-Aunt Bey says on the phone to Mom, real early on Sundays when it is good weather. On those Sundays I squirm on my chair in Sunday School and think only about racing home and to change into my shorts and T-shirt, put on my Keds, and leave our house with all the dumb Rules. The Farm is big cornfields and a very old brick house that has fancy wooden curlicue stuff at the top, and big windows and three stories. There's also a little stone cottage and a big barn with sheep, cows and chickens. It belongs to Gram and Great-Aunt Bey; they are sisters. They own it because their aunt, a woman who was rich and liked to live in lotsa different places, bought the farm in 1925 for $15,000 dollars, and lived there for about 10 years, until she got tired of it and moved to California. She gave it to Gram and Great-Aunt Bey. So Gramp decided people—Paul and Trudy—should live in the big house and do the farming, and we get to go out on weekends and play.

Lotsa people are nice to me at the Farm, like Paul who wears a blue shirt with sleeves rolled up and takes us on his tractor, and Trudy who has pointy glasses and comes out of the kitchen in the big house and talks to Mom.

"We're at the big hill," Robbie says when we are almost done with the drive, and I put away my toys because we have to push. "Harder," Dad says. We have passed the endless stream of low-slung, tidy brick ranch houses, some with rows of fields behind them and others with houses next to them and swing sets in the yard. "At the hill" means we are almost there. Robbie and I get to unbuckle so we can stand up and push against the front seat, to help the car go up the hill. "This is so stupid," Betsy says because she's at Skokie Junior High now and says it doesn't matter if we push. I don't like it when Betsy tells Dad stuff is stupid and rolls her eyes. Doesn't she know we need to keep Dad happy?

"Milk, Bruce," Mom says as we drive by the house with all the little windmills and brightly-colored elf statutes in the yard. I want to stop there and see if it is just as magical inside the house as outside, but we never do. At a little store at the corner, Mom buys milk in a wax paper carton that is red and yellow and that is smaller than the big glass bottles of milk the milkman delivers at home.

And then we turn off the big road and Dad drives up the windy gravel driveway and there is the cottage. Robbie and I run up the three steps and wait; we are always the first to arrive and Mom has to find the key under the big gray stone. I think Dad is cleaning any dirt from our car.

"It's musty," Mom always says. I wonder what musty is but I knew musty will go away soon. Right away I sit in the wicker rocking chair next to the wood stove because after dinner me and Robbie will fight about the chair. After I sit there, I can go anywhere.

My sister, some fifty-five years later, becomes the lucky heir to this commodious wicker rocking chair with its deeply recessed, wide seat and deep back, and in my frequent visits to her I shut my eyes, rock deeply and drift back to 1962.

Everything inside the two-bedroom stone cottage stays the same during my childhood. In the big wicker rocker, I can see the two green couches in the living room, forming an L, which are really beds, but have big cushions against the wall so you think they are couches. There is a big record player that you wind up, and a cabinet with books, and lots of old, old dishes on a shelf with a long table to eat at. Next to the rocker is a closet with big, clunky, wooden doll furniture in a red-polka-dot vinyl bag. There is also a bedroom with a big bed and another one with a bed with kites spread all over it and a bathroom with a door that goes to the attic.

The first thing to do at the Farm is chase the sheep. Betsy and Robbie run into them all clumped together, and if I don't go with them, they laugh at me for being scared so I always hope we chase the sheep first. Dad doesn't go to the sheep and the barn with us, I think because he just wants to be outside, but when we walk through the woods to the really cold brook he comes with us. My other cousins are too little to walk to the brook, so it is just us. I wonder if Dad misses the golf course, because it is Sunday afternoon and instead, he is at the Farm with us. I don't ask him. The afternoon sun is hot on my shoulders and I strip off my T-shirt. Robbie and I plunge our arms to the bottom of the brook to move big stones. We are making a dam; Dad breaks big tree branches on his knee. The mud squishes through our toes making murky bubbles at the water's surface. "If you step over there," Robbie says, pointing to a deeper part of the brook shaded by trees, "you'll get sucked up all the way. It's quicksand!" I look at the shady patch of the brook he is pointing to, and then at Dad. "Really?" I ask, looking at Dad. "Uh-uh," Dad says quietly, intent on breaking particularly tough branches. I let the mud squish up to my knees, and I know I am safe. A watercolor of me, painted from a photo, freezes that moment. My plastic barrette has fallen out of my hair and, happily for me, my brown bangs hang in my eyes. One hand brushes them aside while I peer intently up at Dad. I am knee-deep in the brook, bare chested and smiling.

The brook is the best part of the Farm because Dad is happy there, I think, because there is water, and no golf course to make him get mad if he can't hit the ball very far.

Later, we will hunt for eggs in the haymow, finding rotted, broken ones which prompt us to run down the ladder and out in the fresh air, squealing. At dusk, as I wait for dinner, I walk out past the glider swing in the front yard. It is supposed to be gardens here, except that no one keeps the weeds out anymore, Mom says. So, it is all tall grass, and then a bunch of flowers, and then a path, and I wonder if it looked fancy when Mom was little and visited Aunt Sis at the Farm. I only know Aunt Sis from Gram's photo albums that have crumbly pieces inside when you open them. When I am young, I sprawl on the linoleum floor of the pantry that connects my grandmother's kitchen and formal dining room, with all her albums taken out of the built-in cabinet drawers spread about me.

In the old pictures, Aunt Sis looks nice, but her friend is tall and scary looking. At home we have dress-ups that are funny, pointy grey shoes with really high heels, and fancy purses, and when you open the clasps, you can smell old. Mom says that they were Aunt Sis's, I guess before she came to the Farm. Or maybe when she was done with the outside work, she and her friend put on the shoes with really high heels and walked around the gardens.

There is a picture of a woman of color sitting in a rocking chair in the yard at the Farm, in 1926, with my year-old mother beside her in a playpen. She wears a long white uniform and cap and looks matter of factly at the camera.

Gram has written in her spidery script, "Old Black Mary." Gram told me that Old Black Mary cooked the meals for Aunt Sis and her friend. Aunt Sis and her friend did all the outside work because they liked it.

Years later I scrutinize these albums and ask Mom about the insensitive, quizzical label for Boston-born Mary Powell, who worked for my Aunt Sis in Boston and then moves with her to the farm. In a studio photo taken thirty-four years earlier, in 1892, Mary sits with an infant on her lap—my great Uncle Rick (the nephew of Aunt Sis). He is dressed in a long white baptismal gown, and she wears a long black dress with an embroidered, and highly starched, white apron covering the full length of her black dress, and a fancy hat on her head. Her smile is fixed, and her eyes seem focused on a distant object. My heart wrenches at the thought that she perhaps knew, even then, that caring for this infant was the closest she would come to motherhood. I find that the photo was taken in a studio in Savannah, Georgia, by a photographer who documented "the lives of the black sharecroppers and the day-to-day activities of this region," according to the Georgia Historical Society. The photographer "provides us with the unsentimental view of the South he experienced during the late 1880s and early 1890s."

No one knows why Mary Powell and my great uncle, the infant, were in Savannah at that time. I like to speculate that it was an extended family gathering, and that the photographer, William Wilson, meets Mary and wants to document her role.

Mom shrugs sadly when I point out the "Old Black Mary" label in the 1926 photo. She is hard pressed to remember Mary's last name; I find it under another picture.

I can learn so little of Mary's past. I want to find living relatives of Mary Powell. She was born in Boston in 1870, one of five daughters. At a young age she begins working for my relatives, the Hall family, in Boston. In a photo dated 1880s, she looks like a carefree teen with a brilliant smile, save for the apron tied about her waist. In 1925, she accompanies my great-great aunt to Dundee, IL., to help her run the 20-acre crop farm. Did she have a choice? My mother tells me that by 1950 when she can no longer work, she is "placed" with an family of color in Evanston, who is paid to care for her, and she remains there until she dies. Neither my mother, nor anyone else, knows any more about her.

I can't find an obituary. It's as if this tall, stately woman who posed in photos as a nanny, lost her identity when she went to work for my relatives. How old was she? Did she keep in touch with her four sisters? Did she have a choice about moving 1,000 miles away from her home town when she was 45 years old? I so want to give these photos of her to someone who loved her.

I think Dad likes the Farm. He never goes in the little brick cottage where my mom and aunts make dinner, and where I play in my favorite corner behind the wood stove in the quiet moments after our meal. I can hear murmurs of talk as the women wash dishes in the big porcelain sink, wipe them with faded, checkered dish towels and place them in the oak-paneled, glass-fronted cabinet in the small, narrow kitchen.

My uncles Tom and George fly kites with my cousins in the afternoon, walk the rows of newly planted corn with Paul and sip from cold bottles of Schlitz beer while they prod and cajole lumpy bricks of charcoal into glowing embers and tend to quartered chicken parts, joking, squinting into the sky, and manhandling the chicken parts with a long-handled, two-pronged fork when fat drips onto the burning embers, sending up a burst of flame.

Dad watches, and jokes with them, and relaxes on the back porch, as well, to watch the sun setting in the west.

For a little while, I have the Watervale Dad at the Farm.

When I am a child the Farm is simply an escape from suburban claustrophobia and telephones and televisions. It is not where Mary answered to her name with "Old Black" placed before it, or where Alice Moor drove out with my grandparents in the 1940s, white uniform folded on her lap, to help serve July fourth parties for their Evanston friends.

Alice stands near the simple wooden dining room table, placed outside in the front yard of the Farm, in a 1940 photo. Eight people are seated about it. She is serving them.

In November, 1968, Rob and I have one last, brief overnight trip to the farm with Mom. She helps Great-Aunt Bey sort through chests full of Aunt Sis's clothing and belongings in trunks in the big house. It is time to sell the farm; the Meadowdale International Raceway, built just beyond its borders, intrudes on our visits, with rumbling engines and screeching tires, and Gramp fears encroaching development will further decrease its beauty. It is sold in the beginning of 1970 for $60,000.

I am 11, too young to want to spend any time in this nearly century-old house with its richly varnished butternut and mahogany woodwork; trunks full of mementos left by my eccentric great-great-aunt; and full of memories Mom could have shared with me, had I asked. Rob and I have been granted a treasured day free from school, to glimpse the Farm one last time, and we chose to tromp through the now-empty barn, visit the stream, and stretch our boundaries to a neighboring gravel pit. Mom is no doubt consoling my Great-Aunt Bey over the loss of the family farm.

I lost a little piece of Dad with the sale of that Dundee farm; a piece of the fun Dad—the Watervale Dad—who could break sticks over his knee for our dams, watching us squish warm mud through our toes, and simply Be. And not Do.

CHAPTER SEVEN
"Uncle Dick Wears Cowboy Boots"

"No problem," Lisa says to me one day after school. We're in Mrs. Risch's fourth-grade class, together this year. "I know where we can get money."

"There's lots up on the tracks" she adds, flinging off her bright blue plastic headband and throwing it on the ground. "My brothers showed me how to get it."

Lisa is my new "try-to-keep-up-with-friend"—my friend with a sense of danger—and I am drawn to her with a fascination and giddiness. She has two older brothers in high school, a dad who always travels, and she lives two blocks from White's Drug Store. I have never gone to White's on my own, and anyway we are not allowed to spend our allowance on candy.

"Can ya believe how mad Mrs. Risch got after lunch?" Lisa says as we walk the half block to my house. "She blew up!"

It is a moment forever emblazoned in my brain. After lunch we have returned to school and are "settling," as teachers call it, into our seats in our mobile classroom (Greeley is bulging at the seams in the mid 1960s with post-WWII children) when Mrs. Risch's teacher eyes spot new drawings on the covers of a few of the boys' social studies workbooks.

"Do you boys have *any* idea what that means?" Her dark eyes flash beneath her coif of black hair. She holds up a workbook with a crisscross of bold, black lines for all twenty-five of us to see. "*Any* idea at all?"

Did we? I don't recall. I had no knowledge of the meaning of the swastika until that teachable moment. With a silenced class, we were told most likely a sanitized version of the Holocaust, the atrocity never mentioned in front of me in Winnetka in the 1960s. Recollections of "the war" were always about our dad's undoubtedly heroic efforts. I try to brave the world of Anne Frank, when I see "The Diary of Anne Frank" in Betsy's room and try to read it, but it is several years before I can face the reality.

Lisa and I want only to erase that dark moment from our minds, and we run to her house after I change, and finally the two blocks to Indian Hill Park where we collapse on the grass and she tells me the plan.

"We just go up the stairs to where you get on the train and there won't be anyone there right now," she tells me matter-of-factly. "Then we'll see the newspaper box, and you just stick your hand in the hole and there's a buncha dimes and nickels!"

The small, round hole in the top of the green wooden newspaper box at the Chicago & Northwestern railroad tracks is exactly the right size for a child's hand. We run up the concrete steps, our canvas Keds darkening from the wet leaves. "No one here," Lisa says, looking both directions.

"The old guy in the station won't know we're up here. Sometimes I go in and lock the bathroom stall doors and go out underneath, and he never hears me."

"Ya sure he won't know?" I say, looking down the long set of concrete stairs. "No. He's old," Lisa laughs. "He can't hear."

The wooden box, painted forest green like my Girl scout uniform, is waist high. It is flat-topped, and hinged, so that the dads getting on the train in the morning can put their fifteen cents in the little hole at the back, lift the top and take a paper.

The dads could just lift up the top and take a paper without putting any money in the hole, I think. I guess they don't do this because they don't want God to be mad at them when they go to church on Sunday.

The money is contained in a metal box, and Lisa reaches her hand in and pulls out a fist full of coins.

"See?" she says smiling. "Now you try."

We fly back down the stairs, with change stuffed in our pockets. The bell above the door of White's Drug Store chimes, and as we stand in front of the candy display, I realize I can buy just about anything I want. Quickly I choose a 3 Musketeers, Hot Tamales, a Baby Ruth, Chuckles and five pieces of Bazooka, and hand over forty-five cents. I am scared this money will vanish.

We lay on our backs at the park, and I offer Lisa my licorice Chuckles. "Can I hide the Hot Tamales at your house?" I ask, as I stuff all the bubble gum in my mouth. "I'm not allowed candy."

We steal like this after school, most days, for two weeks, until Lisa says now we need to just take the candy from the store. "It'd be more fun, and my brother says it's easy," Lisa tells me when we meet at the swings after school.

Is risk-taking a genetic trait? I think so. When my daughter bungles her knee—and soccer season—by cliff-jumping on the shores of Lake Champlain at age 17, I understand. When I am asked, as a young reporter in Kenosha, Wisconsin, to visit a nudist colony for a feature article, I don't hesitate to participate. Stealing candy from White's Drug Store, at 9 years old, thrills me.

It is the sharp eyes of the pharmacist/owner the next afternoon that ends our lark. I feel his hand on top of mine, in an almost kindly way, as I try to slide a Slo Poke into my pocket. I cry, immediately and freely. Lisa is next to me.

"In here," he says, guiding us into his crowded office. He stands in his white, high-collar, starched pharmacists' shirt, the double row of buttons gleaming, and makes us sit. I am afraid this dad-like man will punish us.

I can't stop crying, but Lisa stands with her hands in her jacket pockets and her head high. Clearly, she has faced danger before.

It's my crying, I think, that saves us from this be-spectacled store owner's calling our moms. "I've never seen you do it before," he tells us solemnly. "You both need to promise me you will never do it again."

My stealing with Lisa ends that day and I find that eating bowls of ice cream while watching "Dark Shadow" after school in her living room is equally exciting; I am allowed neither at my home after school. A week later Mom is reading the Sunday Tribune in the kitchen. Our kitchen is small, lunch is over, and she is alone in one of the two comfortable chairs she has for her and Dad. I must have gleaned something from Sunday School that morning because I run to her and tears and words spill out.

"It just happened," I say I leave out the worst of our thievery spree—our two days of stealing from White's—and focus on the newspaper box thefts. Of course, we agree Dad doesn't need to know and she loans me three dollars—the amount I am guessing I took in change (perhaps I still owe more, but my recent letters to the tribune go unanswered). I must mail the three dollars, along with a letter explaining my transgressions.

I pay Mom back with my 25 cents weekly allowance.

God pays me back with forgiveness.

In 1965 I was called a tomboy, and I want only to wear jeans and T-shirts and ride my bike and wrestle on the grass with my brother and my friends and swing on the rings at Greeley School playground. I beg Mom, when I am seven years old, to let me become a boy, but she simply says I will be glad, one day, that I am a girl.

And sexuality does awaken in me; Allison and I lie on our stomachs on the swings at Greeley and twist around and around and watch the boys shimmy up the rope, and I get a warm feeling in my tummy. I like to watch those boys.

When I am eight, I invite seven friends to my house on a hot September Saturday to celebrate my birthday, and I stand, before the party starts, in my gift of a cowboy suit—long-sleeved brown checked shirt with snap buttons, whipcord pants that bag at the knees and over my black cowboy boots and a fringed, tan buckskin jacket. I am OK, at this age, pretending to be a cowboy, and yet so happy to get gifts of Barbie doll clothes.

That fall, Robbie wants to move out of the bedroom we have shared. Our twin beds are under the six windows looking out into our tiny strip of a backyard, and in the summers, Mom moves the beds so we lay lengthwise under the windows. On hot summer nights Robbie and I lie on our tummies and put the small plastic cars we'd found on the beach on the window sills, running them back and forth. We found the red and green cars at the foot of a slide on the beach on the Fourth of July, and we agreed if they were still there, unclaimed, the next morning we would take them. Those magical nights disappear that fall with Rob's move to the small "maid's room" off the kitchen.

The week before I turn eight, I discover a present I so very badly want. It is a Sunday and we are driving home from a family birthday party at my grandparents' farm. Dad says we have to stop and meet one of his new salesmen and his family. I am swept away into a new world. This salesman's daughter has a Charmin' Chatty.

I do not want to leave. This doll, with its permanent upturned lips and silky brown hair, means I can be a mother and have a friend who does everything I say. The twenty-inch plastic doll is topped by evenly-parted straight brown hair and anchored with white plastic saddle shoes and it lets me be the mom I want to be. The Mattel doll comes with small round discs to be inserted in her back; she chatters away in my pretend world.

Every night that long, long week, I lie awake, wondering if Mom will buy me Charmin' Chatty. I want two gifts so very badly—a cowboy suit and a doll.

I am a girl but I must do lots of boy things for Dad to love me. My friend Joan tells me that if I sleep on my stomach, I will stop my breasts from developing, and I am excited that I have a solution to what I see as simply a pending disaster. How will I hug the football to my chest if I have THOSE in the way? Dad always says to hug the football real hard when he throws it at us to catch. I want to be on a sports team and have a uniform, but I can only look longingly at Robbie's flannel Little League baseball uniform with its bright red number seven on the back.

I rip the wrapping paper off the rectangular box on my birthday and see the plastic face with bright blue eyes looking at me through the cellophane box. I dress her, place six-inch round discs into the slit in her back, and pull the strings to engage the tiny record player embedded within. "Play with me, feed me, take me with you," the electronic, high-pitched little girl voice sings out. The doll even has a unique smell; a refreshing whiff of new plastic that suspends the reality of school number lines and cleaning the car.

The summer after fourth grade, I tear through the thick brown packing paper on a Sears and Roebuck package, lift the two-piece turquoise blue bathing suit out of its tissue paper nest, and hug it to my nine-year-old flat chest. "It's here," I say breathlessly into the phone, as soon as I have dialed Lisa's HI-6 number. "Meet me at the beach."

This is my very first two-piece bathing suit—"Fun-in-the-Sun Togs for Girls,"—the 1966 Spring/Summer Sears and Roebuck catalog says. Big, round red cherry Popsicle drips stain the page that I show to Mom a million times before she says, "OK"

"Back later," I say as I run upstairs to change. "Going to the beach with Lisa."

Mom looks up. She is writing bills at the kitchen table. "Just don't show it to your father until I tell him," she says.

Two-pieces, my Mom-who–knows-nothing says, are for teenagers and not for nice girls my age.

This aqua bathing suit with its white trim is perfect; no more hot, scratchy one-piece suit that makes me feel like my body is all scrunched inside it. This suit is just like the catalogue says: surfer shorts with elastic on the waist, a zipper and patch pocket and a top that buttons in the back. And the color blue that makes you think of sunshine and bright, sparkly swimming pools.

The two-piece suit is all about no more day camps, but instead stealing the life guards sack lunches at the beach with Lisa and going to visit my cousins in Colorado for two weeks. My memory of that bathing suit fifty years later is so deep-down-in-my-gut wonderful, that I research on-line and learn that I can see it in the 1966 Spring/Summer catalogue at the nearby Shelburne Museum, in their archives.

I squint into the microfiche machine on page 395 and study the saucy, barefoot model with her two brown braids, and instantly I am nine, coveting the matching surf pants and jacket on another model. The model's shapeless body touts the suit, available in red or turquoise Arnel Triacetate. For

$5.94 plus shipping, I could have a "fun-in-the-sun summer," she seems to taunt me back in 1966, and again, recently.

"Bring an old T-shirt," Lisa says to me the next day on the phone. "And black markers."

Lisa is my friend that I wish, looking back, I do not have to leave when we moved from Winnetka eight months later. She awakened in me an independence; a "who-cares-what-happens" belief that I will fail to nurture during adolescence. No surprise that today she is a highly successful professional photographer.

I bike the three blocks to Elder Lane beach, a beach towel, T-shirt and marker in my basket, my turquoise bathing suit shimmering in the sun, and my red rubber flip-flops on my feet. My chin-length brown hair streams behind me.

"We just go up to the pier," Lisa says to me from our beach towel hangout just feet from the edge of Lake Michigan, "and ask them to sign these shirts. Then we wear them here tomorrow!" Do I want the sun-drenched lifeguards from New Trier High School, sitting along the concrete pier all muscles and hairy legs, to sign Robbie's old T-shirt? I feel quivery excitement in my tummy.

"Ya know what else?" Lisa challenges me as we edge up to the pier, our stick figures lost in a sea of Coppertone-laden toddlers and chatting mothers. "Later we could try to steal their lunches!"

Lisa awakens in me an attraction to the lanky, teenage boys at Elder Lane beach, whistles dangling on their bare chests. Yet hours later, I am quietly content, while another friend Laura and I make "Barbie" homes in the rock garden of my front yard, cherry Fizzies sizzling on our tongues.

It is the summer of '66. It is my summer of Forever when I am finally free of morning day camps making plastic lanyards, singing about ridin forever 'neath the streets of Boston and eating graham crackers; of swim lessons in way-too-cold-in-the-morning Lake Michigan; and of golf lessons at the country club wearing shorts that reach to my knees and standing in a line of kids, the litany of club gripping and swinging not even reaching my ears.

That summer the Beatles will give their last live performance; U.S. planes will begin dropping bombs in Hanoi, and the five-year-old Southern Christian Leadership Council begins to compare the indiscriminate bombing of Vietnam to the racial violence in the U.S.

I am unaware of any of this, and of the tremendous efforts by President Johnson to introduce the Civil Rights Act in 1964. This is wrong. I ask my mother, years later, why she and Dad had not talked about the social upheaval trying to infringe on these baby boomer neighborhoods—on these Greatest Generation dads—and she says they thought everything would die down.

The summer before in 1965, I have just met Lisa. We are playing on her street. "They have to take this man thing out," Lisa says, pointing to the three-foot statue of a colored boy with a big smile, painted in bright colors and holding up a rope. It is right next to where we are selling Dixie cups of lemonade for five cents.

"Why?" I ask.

"The police told them to," Lisa says. "They said that next week when the coloreds come to the Village Green, they'll see these and maybe get mad and do something." She shrugs. In our minds, colored people only come to Winnetka to clean your house. And they never get mad.

Martin Luther King speaks to ten thousand people in Winnetka on July 25, 1965. He is brought to Winnetka by the North Shore Summer Project. A group of concerned parents and clergy, legitimately worried about the lack of diversity on the North Shore, and college student volunteers, have invited Dr. King. His appearance, at the end of a day of rallies, is to a mostly white audience who have waited four hours to hear him. His message is clear: Parents who allow their children to grow up without coming into contact with "colored people" are doing a serious injustice, calling it "the silence of the good people."

The event is the first ever civil rights rally with MLK in an all-white suburb. We are, unfortunately, at Watervale. If there is any event I would like someday to recall to my yet-to-be-born grandchildren, it would be hearing Martin Luther King speak.

This summer I teeter between Barbies and boys—between teasing the bare-chested lifeguards at Elder Lane beach and playing in my rock garden fort in the driveway. I learn that other families live free of lessons and country club golf courses that swallow up entire weekend afternoons. "We'll swim when we're done," Mom says as we are left at the country club pool every Sunday afternoon and I watch them head off to the green carpet of a golf course, the sun shimmering on the still damp, newly-watered golf greens.

The country club is a place that puts more cold, ironclad rules in my nine-year-old life. Years later, my husband will tell me that he gladly would have traded hot summer days weeding rows of tomatoes and beans on his parents' Midwest farm, for Skokie Country Club lessons. In 1965 I only know that these "wear-the-clothes-I-tell-you and this-is-good-for-you" experiences" are excruciating. I know deep down, as I can imagine did other kids who did not want to listen to highly-paid, always-grinning golf pros tell us how to swing a golf club, this is not the reason I am on earth, and why, for heaven's sake, would anyone have kids if they only want them to be themselves all over again?

Does Dad even care what makes me, me?

> "You know June. I think I've learned something from all of this; to take our kids as they are—not wish they were something else or try to make them like ourselves. It doesn't work."
>
> Ward to June. "Part time Genius," season 1, episode 14.

Dad travels during the week, beginning that summer, and there is a chink in the armor of Mom and Dad's well-oiled, tightly-controlled Winnetka household. It is unraveling, and I flourish in the freedom. I win the two-piece argument, and many others that spring of 1966, and with his travel, summer evenings of Dad's ball-throwing and relay races with the neighbors end.

"Throw it harder," Dad says to my dark-haired, next-door neighbor Mary as she tosses the softball back to Dad. We are standing on the small strip of grass between the sidewalk and the street at the end of the driveway and the sun is setting. "I can't," objects Mary. She has no dad living at her house, so when we play catch out here, instead of the front lawn, she always comes over. "You want to throw it harder than everyone else," Dad says to us. "You want to be the best."

Robbie becomes Rob that summer and is gone from our front yard, off to camp or on his purple Schwinn ten-speed, pedaling throughout the North Shore. My sister leaves for a long summer of camp.

I am, as a writer now, drawn to remember the most minute of details. When I can recall the age I was when I trotted over to a friend's house at six a.m. one morning to play, waking their household, or what kind of brown packing box Jimmy and I used to make a desk for him when we are eight, because we thought that he was going to be a famous writer, I feel alive and certain of my place in the world.

Later, at a PR job, I would expect an instantaneous raise when I include, in a news release, the high school mascot of a soon-to-be-well-known surgeon. (Pre-internet days, this requires a phone call and inquiry). I am a collector of moments of the past.

On a hot July afternoon, that summer of 1966, I am free to bike to Elder Lane beach to play. I go alone, an uncommon occurrence, as Winnetka is filled with my friends. I wheel my Schwinn into the bike rack and go down the stone steps to the beach. I am too old for the playground and I will use this treasured free summer afternoon to read a book and swim.

I am good at playing alone, and I don't notice the slender, chestnut-haired girl watching me at first. Finally, she comes into the water and dog paddles to the waist-deep water where I am practicing the log rolls Betsy is learning in water ballet at New Trier. "I'm Jennie," she says, her long hair fanning out as she kneels in the water. "That's my gramma back on the beach." Jennie points to a woman with her eyes shaded looking toward the water. "Can we play?"

This memory is seared into my mind. I teach her how to do log rolls, point out which lifeguards are cutest, and later I bike to her gramma's house, five blocks from mine, and we sit on her back porch and eat Windmill cookies and talk. Or maybe play cards.

I look for Jennie the next afternoon at the beach. She is not there.

I think God sent her to me to let me know I am OK.

On the train to Colorado Springs, Uncle Dick wears cowboy boots.

I cannot stop staring at his brown leather, pointy-toe boots coming out from underneath his khaki suit. I only know dads to wear cordovan wingtips with suits.

He chuckles, his bushy blond mustache dancing and his blue eyes light up. He has taken me and my cousins Steph and Cate, who are nine and ten, to the observation car while Aunt Judy and Matt read a book in our sleeper. I am going to visit my cousins for two weeks.

"They're not just for riding," he explains to me when I ask why he is wearing them. "You're going to the West, Emily."

This is not my first long train trip, but it is my first one without Mom telling me what to do and with no Rules from Dad. "Climb on up," Uncle Dick says while he holds back to help the porter with the suitcases, and urges us up the steep stairs leading to the train car. It is fun to sit in our compartment with big seats and eat sandwiches in a brown paper bag from my grandmother.

I suspect it was my very kind Aunt Judy who invited me to visit them for two weeks in their Colorado Springs home. I had been there once before, with my whole family, and in my mind there is nothing better than living near horses and mountains and an uncle who wears cowboy boots and owns a bookstore. I give short shrift that summer to my Aunt Judy, I am afraid, who I now realize spent those two weeks juggling four young children and her work in the growing bookshop.

My Great-Aunt Bey has given me a dollar to buy anything I need for this trip, and I must make three trips to Charley's Variety Store on my red Schwinn before I am able to pick out a plastic, purple-flowered, zippered case for my comb, toothbrush and toothpaste. I am very ready to venture beyond life in Winnetka and live with an uncle who reads books all day and wears cowboy boots to work.

Uncle Dick has built a treehouse in the side yard and

a big three-story dollhouse that is painted fancy and he takes us horseback riding and hiking. Plus it is very fun to visit where he works. The only fun thing, ever, about seeing where Dad works is the vending machine and the chairs at the desks, without arms, that we can wheel across the floor. Secretaries chairs, Dad calls them.

"Any book I want?" I look up at my Uncle Dick, and see his bright blue eyes twinkling. "Any book," he replies.

I turn to Cate and Steph. "My very own book?" I ask, for reinforcement. We are in Uncle Dick's bookstore, and I know it will take me forever to pick out a book I get to keep. I think that Cate and Steph must spend all their free time here, around all these books and their dad who is always happy.

Steph flashes her grin and starts climbing up in the playhouse nestled in the corner of the children's section. The monkey house, they call it, and in it are big, comfy pillows to sit on while you read. Uncle Dick built it, just like the tree house, and the dollhouse he made out of packing boxes and painted with red curlicues on the outside.

Colorado Springs is the bookstore, and playing in the tree house, and having bright sunshine every single day. I don't know if Dad smiles all day like Uncle Dick does in his bookstore.

I am homesick only once and it is because it feels strange to live without so many Rules. My cousins and I are at the grocery store with my aunt; my youngest cousin Matt is home. We are nearly done with the shopping, and Steph tells me I can pick out a candy bar. Any candy bar.

"A whole one just for me?" I ask.

"Yep," blond-haired Steph shakes her head earnestly. "Any candy bar that costs a dime."

Mom has bought me candy bars very rarely in my life. Once, after we had a car accident and we all had to wait two hours while the car was fixed, we got to buy Hershey bars out of the gas station vending machine. Sometimes on the car ferries she lets us buy a Nestle Crunch out of the vending machine.

Buying a candy bar is a very big deal, and I pick out a 3 Musketeers bar and clutch it in my hand, relishing the thought of a whole candy bar to myself, after dinner. I will eat it in the tree house, I decide, and pretend I live here.

"What'd ya get?" Steph asks me from the back seat of the station wagon, as she unwraps her Baby Ruth. I wipe the sweat off the back of my thighs which are sticking to the vinyl car seat. "3 Musketeers," I say. "We can eat them now?

"Sure," Steph says. "Just don't leave the wrapper in the car."

The chocolate and fluffy filling trickle down my throat; I have never been allowed to eat a candy bar in the car, or near dinner time.

It is delicious.

That night, as I lay in the twin bed next to my cousin Cate, my happy feeling slips away and I begin to cry, silently. I am remembering when I used my allowance to bring home a candy bar, on a Saturday, and Mom saw it in my jacket pocket. I had to throw it away.

Do my cousins get to have candy when they want it, I wonder? Do some moms even buy bubble gum? It is heaven, when I go to a birthday party or on Halloween, and get Bazooka bubble gum. The soft pink gum feels squishy between my teeth, and a lovely sugary sweetness goes down my throat. So I look for Robbie's discarded pieces of bright pink gum on our front walk, and rinse them under the faucet and make it my own gum.

I don't know how to live without Rules, I think, as the tears run down my cheeks.

"What is that curvy thing sticking out in back of me?" I wonder, when I get home and look at my side profile. Last summer I didn't have a curvy butt, I tell myself. I don't want my butt to stick out like the red rubber ball we use for kickball at Greeley. This curvy part of me is going to get in the way when I try to wear Rob's blue jeans, or we squish our hips together to share the brown chair in front of the TV.

When my photo is taken that fall—by the same commercial photographer who takes our photos every fall—a too-sweet white-haired woman with black Harlequin glasses—I am looking into the camera with a shy, happy look. I am relaxed. A year later, she is unable to capture a natural smile.

The evening is hot in late August, when Mom, Dad and Rob and I ride in our brown Skylark convertible to the Winnetka Community House. I am excited; Betsy is coming home from camp. Rob is quiet, but I know that he, too, feels glad that all five of us will be together again; that on a weeknight, we will all go to the Sweet Shop for ice cream.

My sister is a summer camp person. She loves the giddiness of girls eating meals together; the challenge of week-long canoe trips, and the mornings spent weaving key chains and learning J strokes. She arrives on the bus that evening full of jokes only she and her best friend, Margo, understand, and a new-found reserve for us, her family.

The orb of street light shines on my blue shorts, checkering them a bright green as we sit on benches and I lick my fudge ripple ice cream. I remember only the strangeness of how the street light changed the color of our clothes, and the sweet, chilled ice cream sliding down my throat, a rare weeknight treat.

I don't remember Mom saying, that evening, "We're moving."

I don't remember Mom's telling us that Dad has a new job, and we will move to Battle Creek. I don't remember Dad's saying that he will start the job in September and he will travel even more and that we will move after Christmas.

I don't remember thinking I will be leaving my friends Laura and Lisa, and there will be no more bike rides to Elder Lane beach. No more biking all over Winnetka on streets where I know the best trick-or-treating, and the biggest October bonfires of leaves. No more thin white T-shirts to wear with our cut-offs, with Mike and Dave and Stan written in black magic marker. No more stealing lifeguard lunches and giggling in the woods as we eat their Hostess Twinkies.

The Summer of Forever is ending. I want to hold onto my turquoise two-piece bathing suit; my horseback rides with Uncle Dick under the hot Colorado sun and the magic of a street light turning my shorts to blue-green as I lick my fudge ripple ice cream cone.

But my suit will go in the Goodwill box that fall. "It won't fit next summer," Mom says. So, too, will my stuffed pink poodle dog with a blue checkered vest that I win at Riverside Amusement Park, and my Creepy Crawler set and my Barbie and her playhouse.

It is an end.

CHAPTER EIGHT
"Do-Over"

When?" he asks, "did *this* happen?"

Dad's hand goes rigid on my back and he pulls it away, shifting his weight away from me on our porch glider, as if I am on fire. I redden, as if the cool September evening air on our enclosed porch has become hellishly hot, and I sit as if paralyzed. The blue-and-green-flowered-vinyl glider cushions are sticking to my thighs and I feel like if I just don't move maybe Dad will suddenly understand.

But he doesn't.

"A bra?" Dad looks at Mom with furrowed brow. She is in a raffia woven porch chair, stitching Betsy's name on her gym suit. The white threaded needle goes in and out of the blue cotton. She looks at Dad. "Yes," she says.

A week before the start of fifth grade, Mom tells me it is time to wear a bra. I stand on a chair in my sister's room next to her closet and reach high up in her closet and take out the box of hand-me-downs. I love to search through the hand-me-down box for Rob's old T-shirts, but this time Mom pulls out a small pile of Teenform training bras.

"You should start wearing this," she says. "At least by the time school starts."

I try the bra on in my bedroom. It is an unwieldy crisscross of white straps, padded cotton and elastic and I see no reason for it. I shove it into the far reaches of a dresser drawer, until Rob tells me to wear it.

Dad rises from the glider, and it creaks, his shifting weight causing me to swing a bit as I sit with arms folded around my legs brought up to my chest, trying to become as small as I possibly can. Maybe he is remembering all the hot, sun-drenched afternoons on the Lake Michigan beach at Watervale, when I was younger and I could be bare-chested. Dad picks up the Chicago Tribune and goes to the living room, silent.

I run to my bedroom

He doesn't like me this way, but I will wear the bra because Rob told me that girls in fifth grade do that. "Don't ya know the boys try to snap your straps on your back on the playground?" Rob said to me. "If you don't have any straps...."

I know stuff is going to happen to my body. It's dumb; I like my body just the way it is. Way back in second grade I learned that my body's going to change. "Do ya know what that is?" My friend Joan, whose mother lets us have Jay's potato chips every time I go there for lunch, finds me in my hiding spot in the far reaches of Mom's closet during hide and seek. Because our house was built by an architect, for himself, it is full of way-high-up cabinets and has big closets and is the best house on my street for this game. Joan has pointed to a large cardboard box with blue and white flowers on it. "No," I say. "We're gonna bleed," she says, and pulls out a thick pad of cotton from the open box. "Down here." She points between her legs.

I don't believe her, even if her sister who is way older than mine and already at New Trier, told her.

I will mature early, beginning menstruation on a cold February Saturday afternoon when I am 11. I am at my friend Tory's house, and I tell her I have to go home because I have a stomachache. We are cutting out photos of Barry Williams from Tiger Beat magazine. At home, when I show Mom the blood on my underpants, I am dreading her explanation.

Mom tells me not to worry about Dad's reaction and that he just doesn't want to see me grow up because I am the youngest. But I worry that he will only love me if I can be like a boy. I don't want breasts, or hips, or to have to wear dresses to school and church.

That fall, I start my seventh and final year at Greeley, nested in the second-floor classroom of longtime-fifth-grade teacher Louise Warwick. While she is the toughest teacher I will have at Greeley, I am in a class filled with classmates I have traversed the wide hallways with since I was four years old.

I am with my tribe.

I, too, am nested at our house on Fairview Avenue. We have outgrown this quirky little brick house. I have moved my twin bed down to the back "maid's room" off our kitchen, a tiny enclave separated from the laundry area by a squeaky accordion door. One wall is full of cabinets, and it is here Mom stores seasonal items, so I have only a bed and a dresser and small closet. But it is mine, and when Laura and I run to my bedroom after school, escaping taunts or misunderstood teasing from the boys we have known since kindergarten, we lie on my bed and pull from underneath it my box of trolls. Whatever game we devise in the peaceful security of my small bedroom has us holding our stomachs in laughter. We regain our balance—our strength—and are ready to face, again, the barrage of teasing boys and new admonishments, every day from Mrs. Warwick, which we need to prep ourselves for the academic rigors of Skokie Junior High. "Next fall," she says, "you'll be in a new school and need to be ready for much more work."

But I am never to enter the monolith brick building that Betsy and Rob have somewhat mysteriously disappeared to every school day for the past four years. All I know about Skokie is that you ride a bus, the boys care about how the girls dress, you have to do reports, and you eat in a cafeteria.

We are moving, right after Christmas. Dad is already working in Battle Creek and just coming home on weekends. Word among the corporate executive wives is that it is easier to settle your kids in a new town during the school year, so it is decided we will move mid-year.

I want a do-over. I want to be in the class photo of all those kids I have known since I started Greeley a few weeks before my fourth birthday. I want to do the fifth-grade class play, attend the fifth-grade "goodbye" ceremony, and I want to know if Paul, the tow-headed, bespectacled boy with a grin so wide it must have hurt, was going to become my fifth-grade boyfriend.

I want to know so badly that my heart aches.

"Do-over, do-over," the kid whose fist who ends up last in our "my-mother-says-to-pick-the-very-best one" selection process for team selection would plead. If the "loser" could garner enough support we'd thrust our fists back in a circle and begin our chant anew.

I want a do-over of fifth grade at Greeley School. Here is what I miss when we move:

Sarah, Laura, Lisa. I already write letters to Joan because she moved right after fourth grade. The creaky floors. The creaks always make me feel like something wonderful is going to happen.

The red stone drinking fountain in the courtyard where Chessie will stand on her hind legs to drink from. Really. It is against a wall, and has a kicking horse carved into it.

Red kick balls and Mr. Kryda pitching them just right for kickball.

My desk that has a top you can move to three different angles.

Paul, who I sorta like.

Writing with really soft chalk.

The library the most, after Sarah, Laura and Lisa. In fifth grade you can be in the library club and put away books.

Cleaning erasers with the machine in the basement with Mr. Marinelli.

The rings to swing from on the playground.

The red things with rubber mallets in music class.

The school picnic and free ice cream.

Walking to school and home with Laura all the time because she passes right by my house. I miss that the very most.

When I finally visit Greeley, shortly after my fiftieth birthday, I wanted to just sit in my old fifth-grade classroom. Mrs. Warwick's old classroom was on the second floor, in the northeast corner of the building and I was once again running into the side playground entrance and up the stairs to be on time. It was spring break so the building was nearly empty and if I shut my eyes, I was awash in the love of my best friends, Sarah and Laura. Sarah, who I began playing with when we were three, in junior kindergarten, is becoming my very best friend in fifth grade, and when I leave in February, after almost seven years with her, I feel limp and hollow.

From my fifth-grade classroom I can see Art the Mailman's corner, my brother's best friend's house, and the school entrance where my sister was featured in a home movie taken on her first day of school, in 1955.

When I am in fifth grade, we are the big kids of this multi-storied, sprawling red brick school and have played on every inch of its playground.

That fall, I hold a birthday party at the Farm. Lisa, Laura, Sarah and I tumble out of the brown Skylark convertible, our hair tossed wild by the hour-long drive, and giggle our way to the front door of the small cottage.

"Twister first," Lisa shouts, brushing blond strands of hair out of her face. She struggles up the cottage steps with her sleeping bag, pillow, birthday gift and duffel. "After we make sleeping places."

"No," I say. "Chasing the sheep is first."

On this Friday evening in late September we arrive with Mom and Betsy as the sun is setting behind the small stone cottage. I don't know this is to be one of my last visits to the Farm, and that, within three years, encroaching development will prompt my grandfather to sell it.

We throw our flannel-lined sleeping bags in the small cottage living room and run down the dirt road to the brick barn. I show them the shadowy hay mow, the bleating sheep, the hike to the brook and the once fancy gardens in the front lawn.

After dinner, and before Twister, we take Mason jars from the dusty, earthen basement and run through the front yard catching fireflies. We are ten, and we don't think of the changes coming to our bodies, friendships and rural Carpentersville. By the time we are teens, the Farm will be sold, I will have lost touch with Lisa, Laura's parents will divorce, and Sarah will be very popular.

That night, all is the same.

That fall and early winter, I am really not aware we are moving. I am so happy with my 10-year-old life, that I only glance at the pamphlet, "Moving made Easy for the Housewife," on Mom's desk. I ignore discussion between Mom and Dad on weekends about their remodeling plans for the house they have found to buy in Battle Creek.

I wonder why I don't object to the gleaning of my childhood stuffed animals, board games and plastic toys, but Mom had always been a sorter. I overhear threads of conversation on our kitchen phone as Mom convinces the Thayer/Lingle relatives to let her host Christmas dinner. "It's our last holiday here," she says. It is a change from the norm, but I am so excited about my new blue and brown plaid hip-hugger skirt that Christmas, I don't think at all of the changes ahead.

That winter, our very demanding, yet highly creative fifth-grade teacher, Mrs. Warwick, tries to prepare me for my mid-January move.

"Aren't we always the last kids to get out for recess and the first to leave?" I ask on the playground one January afternoon as I look up into her eyes—to me they look like hard, blue stones. I wipe my dripping nose with wet wool mittens. We are lined up behind her to return to our classroom.

"If you're dissatisfied with the recess time," Mrs. Warwick says crisply, lowering her half glasses at me, "then you can spend the rest of the afternoon out here." Her sharp tone perfectly matches her precisely-coiffed gray hair. She puts a firm hand on Hughie, the line leader, and leads our class past the kindly eyes of Mr. Kryda.

Sarah and Laura look at me with rounded, disbelieving eyes and even Hughie, who has teased me since second grade for crying in math, shoots me a sympathetic glance with his dark, flashing eyes.

"You can stay outside the rest of the afternoon," Mrs. Warwick calls back to me, as my classmates march like a line of soldiers into the building. "Then you should have plenty of recess."

I stare at the steel gray fortresses of the jungle gym and at the windows of my old kindergarten room. Mr. Kryda is following my class inside. The swings are still and the steel-piped monkey bars—where we climb to the top and taunt the younger kids with "king of the castle, you're the dirty rascals"—seem to dare me to scramble on them and try to play alone. This playground is where I grew up; where Robbie and I ran after Saturday chores to play with neighborhood kids; where we reveled in the freedom from the classroom.

Now it is scary.

Fat tears roll down my face and my shoulders heave. The grayness of the day seems to suffocate me. I think of running down the block to my house, burrowing away in the safe haven of my bedroom. But I want to be where I am supposed to be, where I belong. Under these skies steely gray and in the frigid air, I am alone. And in two weeks we are moving.

> "I don't think going to a new school is so neat, Beav," Wally says to Beaver after Ward tells them he has made an offer on a new house. "What's going to happen when you move away and lose all your friends?" he later asks Ward.
>
> "Beaver Says goodbye," season 2, episode 15.

"Gee whiz Dad, I don't want to move," Beaver says. "I like this house. I've got all my friends here in Mayfield."

"I've been hard on you because it's going to be different at your new school," Mrs. Warwick says on my last day, taking me aside in the hallway. "I want you to be prepared. You'll find not every school is like Greeley." She lowers her half glasses, and smiles, almost kindly, and I stand obediently. I want to turn and walk away but her firm hand is on my shoulder. "Just be ready for a change," she intones, and trods on her crepe-soled shoes back into the classroom.

There are so many good things about fifth grade that I don't want to leave. We know exactly what time to leave the playground to make it to class on time, before school and at lunch. I am a library assistant, I can come home for lunch without Mom being there, and Sarah says Paul in my class likes me.

Within this massive brick structure with its turret atop the front entrance, I struggle mightily with math workbooks, number lines, and the loss of my best friend Allison, after third grade, but I thrive with the familiarity of Brad teasing me, Hughie laughing at our confusion over Jewish holidays and Mr. Kryda's telling the girls we can throw a ball just as far as the boys.

Though I will hate staying after school nearly every Friday afternoon in fifth grade to try to work my way through two years of math workbooks, I can recall, very fondly, Mrs. Warwick's creativity in the classroom and on the day Sarah and Laura and I lift our puppet-covered arms to the classroom puppet stage and waggle the puppets' Styrofoam ball heads, I am excited.

"The funny guy, the funny guy, here comes the funny guy." I singsong the line from my favorite Grace Allen Hogarth book and elbow Sarah to raise her puppet and a couple of boys seated near the puppet stage start laughing. We have done two puppet shows for our book project and each time the boys laugh.

My fifth-grade world is just about perfect.

"You can't ask," Laura says brashly, then looks down at her feet, suddenly quiet. It is my last day at Greeley and Laura, picking me up after lunch, carries a grocery bag.

"Just, what's in it?" I prod as we walk down the slushy-covered sidewalk.

"I can't tell, so just don't ask, but we have to walk fast. We have to get there," Laura says. Laura walks fast, and bunches the front of her jacket together, where the zipper is broken. Laura's mom is the only mom I know who doesn't fix clothes, or other stuff. She doesn't say anything when I go to Laura's house, and smokes cigarettes with her long, dark hair hanging in front of her face.

"Yeah, but I won't tell," I say, quickening my pace.

"If I tell you," Laura says to me, "You gotta act surprised. You gotta."

Laura looks down at her feet. We keep walking.

This is the last time I will walk to school with Laura, but I will cry if I think about that. "What is it?" I try again.

"I have ice cream, for a party, for you. It's a surprise and you can't tell anyone that I told you." Laura tells me quickly and looks up at me and smiles. "It's gotta be a surprise."

She raises her head so she can see past her blond bangs.

"O.K?"

I try very hard not to smile when Mrs. Warwick sends me to the office, an hour later, to get a box of pencils. I walk down the quiet hallways in my very favorite school clothes—my brown hip-hugger skirt with blue stripes and my blue angora sweater. Sarah had to work very hard to convince her mom it is OK for her to wear a hip hugger skirt; we both got them for Christmas.

I try so very hard to act surprised when Sarah meets me at the classroom door and yells "surprise," and I see bright blue crepe paper hanging from the windows. Hughie yells out "did ya know?" but Mrs. Warwick quickly asks the girls to hand out Dixie cups of Hawaiian Punch and sends Hughie to get the ice cream from the nurse's office.

Sarah hands me a big roll of thick white paper tied up with a gold cord. "It's a scroll," she says. I untie the cord and hold the gold spray-painted dowel rods and unwrap the fancy paper. Messages from all my classmates are written in blue fountain pen.

" You are my best friend since second grade and I will visit you," Laura had written in a firm, bold print. "Don't forget me."

I don't forget anyone.

"Did Laura tell you?" Hughie asks me after the party, as I put my gym shoes and art shirt into a brown paper grocery bag to take home.

" No," I lie. I don't think Laura is going to be OK without me; she needs me to be her friend, and I know Hughie will tell Jim and the other boys, and they will be mean to her. And already some girls can't go to her house anymore since her dad moved out of their house and to an apartment in Chicago.

I don't stay close to Laura; we only write letters for a few months, and when I go to visit Sarah in the summers, I don't see Laura. Three years later I am visiting during the week and attend a day of eighth grade with Sarah. During gym class, I stand at the edge of the gym, while the class plays volleyball. "Emily!" Laura says to me when sees me, and smiles shyly.

"Hi," I say quietly. I turn away and go to the drinking fountain. Sarah and Laura are no longer friends, and my 13-year-old self feels I have to choose between them. But there is no choice. Sarah is very popular and already has a boyfriend and has very nice clothes.

That should be a do-over, and if I could make anything happen it would be to apologize to the people I hurt, like Laura, out of utter shyness and lack of confidence.

The fifth-grade class photo, taken one month after I have moved, shows Sarah and Laura standing next to each other, but there is a space next to Sarah. Sarah is looking down while Laura looks expectantly at the camera. I think they saved a space for me.

I want my friends.

My last day at Greeley is a long day of goodbyes, while movers pack all but our beds. We are supposed to move the next day, but an unexpected twenty-three inches of snow begins falling that evening and the blizzard shuts down Chicago—the city will send seventy-five million tons of snow to Florida by train—and delays our move a week. This is not, unfortunately, an extra week to coast down Winnetka's sledding hills with my friends. We are shuttled to relatives in Evanston for the week, and Mom spends hours on the phone rescheduling our move.

That week of limbo in late January, caused by nature's fate, throws all five of us a bit off balance, and the move scheduled for a Friday is reset for eight days later. The new moving company won't transport our four pets, so our departure that Saturday morning is harried. The three cats are hastily confined to a basket which sits in the middle of the back seat. So anxious are my parents to finally move that Betsy, Rob and I somehow end up with a giant bag of M & M's to munch on for the three-hour drive.

Several hours later, when our new neighbors in Battle Creek take Betsy and me to a four p.m. matinee, I feel only glazed and disoriented as our new teenage neighbors and their friends tell me and Betsy all about what radio stations to listen to.

When Monday morning hits, and Mom takes me to Riverside Elementary School, with instructions to ride the bus home, I am riddled with anxiety.

"Her name is Emily and she's from Chicago," my new teacher says as I stand just inside my new fifth-grade classroom. She guides me to an empty desk which is, mercifully, nearby.

Greeley is no more.

CHAPTER NINE

"Milk Bottles"

"Don't go, don't go, DON'T GO."

I squeeze my eyes shut, clench my fists and scrunch my face. Sally's just gotta jump out of the backseat of her dad's station wagon, flick her bangs at me and smile, I think.

But the gravel crunches as her dad backs his green Pontiac out of our driveway, flashes his warm smile from the driver's seat, and heads down the street. Sally puts her head out the window and waves.

I duck my head; I am crying.

I don't want to feel. I hurt, all over, inside and out.

This is depression, I realize a dozen years later when I seek counseling for a similar feeling. It is a black cloud and a heavy weight; an intruder with a determination to settle in. I plunge into its deep, dark depths that early May afternoon. We've lived in Battle Creek for three months and our Watervale friends have visited for the weekend.

"Leaves to rake," Dad says. It is only early afternoon, and the rest of the day weighs heavily because I know all I will think of is how much I miss Sally.

And Sarah. And Laura.

There is little acknowledgement of feelings in our household. There is a "buck up and keep busy" mentality that will keep me going until I leave home and must face my demons.

At lunch, on my first day at Riverside Elementary School, I try to throw away my milk bottle. "It goes in this basket," Terri says, rolling her eyes at me under her long brown bangs. "Right there." She points to a big wire basket with twenty-four little square spaces for our empty bottles. "Didn't you do that at your old school?" She laughs, and tosses back her long hair.

Terri is assigned to be my friend. She is the most popular girl in class because she has a boyfriend and very long hair. "If you hurry," she tells me at lunch where we sit at a round table at the back of our classroom, munching baloney sandwiches, "we can go outside." She smiles and her eyes dance. "We can watch the boys." Jumping rope on the black asphalt outside the school, or watching the boys playing their version of a game with a ball, is how the girls at Riverside spend their recesses or free time after lunch. Because I haven't jump-roped since second grade, and because Terri likes Brian, I follow her into the snowy field and stand, shivering, while we watch the boys.

"Are you a snob? I mean, is that the kind of shoes they wear in Chicago?" Brian asks me that afternoon during PE, pointing at my brown suede Hush Puppies. These are the shoes Sarah and I begged our mothers for, just before Christmas.

How do I answer?

After school, I ride a school bus and it is hot and crowded and I have to stand up and Stuart pushes me over. Because I am new, and he likes me, he tells me, many years later.

It is Riverside Elementary School's big blue lockers that throw me the most. It is not the cursive writing, homework, eating lunch at school, riding a school bus, desperately needing friends, or the much smaller library (indeed, I find many wonderful books in this library) that throw me off kilter, but the large blue lockers embedded in the halls when the school was built in the 1950s.

I am assigned one of these imposing lockers on my first day. These same lockers, from All-Steel Equipment of Aurora, Illinois, are still in the school when I visit 45 years later. In it I must put my jacket, boots, lunch box and gym shoes. For some reason this makes me very sad and seems a huge task, though there are no locks to contend with. I want the coziness of Greeley's "cloak rooms," where we hung our jackets together, shared our secrets and left our wet boots. I miss the intimacy.

> "I was a little worried about how Beaver made out at school today... I'm going to telephone Miss Landers and see if I can pave the way for Beaver," Ward to June. "Would your father have done it for you?" June asks. "Never in a million years. That's why I'm going to do it for Beaver."
>
> "Beaver Becomes a Hero," season 4, episode 3.

Finally, I make a friend. I tell Mom about Barb, who is in my class, and she tells me that Dad says Barb's dad works for him. My mind is exploding, because in Winnetka, no one's dad ever worked for anyone else's dad. I like to go to Barb's house, but it is very small and she shares a bedroom that is so small it has bunk beds, with her little brother.

I am, today, still incredulous that my North Shore-raised parents did not prepare us for a move to Battle Creek. I must add I feel very fortunate to have lived in two very different social environments, and I can't even try to guess if the transition would have been easier, had it been Battle Creek to Winnetka. Probably not. Mom and Dad do not tell my naive self that we will go to school with children of Kellogg's and Post Cereal factory workers, that many houses will be small and tract-built and many people have to stretch a dollar. Battle Creek is terrifically friendly and unassuming, and we live among the lawyers and corporate types in a comfortable house on a lake. My parents thrive here and assume an even busier social life than in Winnetka. I am anchorless and need help with a genetically-inherited depression which I will finally recognize, in my twenties.

As an adolescent, I flounder and flip, fighting with Rob for our ever-increasingly-socially busy mom's attention, and avoiding Betsy's teasing, perhaps a result of her adjusting to a small-town high school after almost two years at bustling, sophisticated New Trier.

In fifth grade, when I ask Barb why she shares a room with her brother, she doesn't ask me to play again for a long time. I blunder with another new friend, when I overhear her mom discussing their mortgage on the phone.

"What's a mortgage?" I ask. I have lived in a privileged world where I don't know people borrow money to buy homes.

My next friend is Becky. Becky's mom always smiles. "You pick the strawberries and we'll make shortcake when you get back," Becky's mom changes from her crisp, yellow Bill Knapp's waitressing uniform into Mom Clothes and sends us four blocks away, beyond the cluster of small post-World War II houses, to a farm to pick berries. It is June, my second summer in Battle Creek, and I have never picked strawberries. Becky shows me how to squat in the sun-drenched field and slip the berry off its stem. Later, I sit at the kitchen table with Becky and her parents and two sisters eating dinner.

Becky's dad smiles and tells me we made good shortcake. It is Saturday evening, and he is relaxed, having the day off from Kellogg's. I didn't know moms and dads eat dinner at home with their kids on Saturday nights.

But I don't belong.

I am spending the night, and on Sunday morning we plan to go to church. Becky's grandmother arrives at the small, three-bedroom, one-story house, to go with us. As I wait in the tiny living room to pile into the family sedan, her grandmother pulls a dollar from her purse to tuck into a pocket. "My offering," she says absently.

I am bursting with confusion. Mercifully, I am smart enough not to say anything.

"One dollar?" I think. "One dollar?" When I sit in church with Baba, in Evanston, he slips a twenty-dollar bill into an envelope and puts it in the gold offering plate.

I am confused. And I hate the country club.

My parents love country clubs. When we move to Battle Creek, the country club is just down the street, and so I have to go to even more lessons because I can walk there. My mother plays golf at the country club quite often.

She has lots of friends there. I don't, because the friends I make at school don't belong to the country club.

I am invited to go to Winnetka to visit Sarah for a week in June. I ask my new friend Barb to help me buy a purse for the trip; she and others in my class have large white purses they carry over their shoulders. We walk several blocks from her house to Shopper's Fair; I carry a month's allowance in my pocket, and I have just enough for a white-vinyl-zippered purse with black stitching on the outside. We can even buy red licorice to eat on the way home.

"Why is it so stuffed looking?" Betsy asks me the next day. "Just stuff I need," I say. "I'm going away for a week."

Betsy is 15 and thinks she is cool. She picks up my purse and empties it.

"It's all Kleenex," she says, laughing, and throwing big wads of tissues on the floor. She also takes out my small coin purse, comb and my paperback book.

I only want to be like everyone else. I want to be like all my classmates at Riverside. I am with those classmates now, and I am no longer with my classmates at Greeley. I know I am different, from the time I walk into the airport at O'Hare where Sarah and her mom meet me, until I am dropped off a week later at my grandparents' house in Evanston.

The Winnetka streets are no longer mine; the Sno Kones at Charles' Variety cost .15 cents instead of .10 cents, and Sarah and I hang out at the country club pool, where Nancy is her new best friend.

Sarah's mom takes us downtown one day and while we are in the shops in Chinatown, I look for a wallet to match my purse. I spy a shiny, white, plastic clutch-style wallet for ninety-seven cents; its very creaminess, shininess and smooth plastic surface appeal to me.

Sarah doesn't laugh at my purse, or my wallet, but I know I am different.

That summer, Mom plays golf, and Betsy and I play Parcheesi in the basement and watch reruns of the Beverly Hillbillies. All summer.

The next summer, the camp routine which I had evaded for two summers, returns.

All I ever want, in the summer, is to get up and put on shorts and a T-shirt, eat my fried egg, and play. If I get tired of playing, I will read a book. I can play for hours, because I am in my own head, and no teacher is telling me what to think or what to do. And I will never, ever get tired of reading a book.

When I am young, I tell Mom that I don't want to go to day camp, and I will go on any errands she wants me to go on, and I will make my own lunch and I will be ready to play any game Dad wants me and Rob to play after dinner on the lawn. I won't cry and go ask to play SPUD in the street with the MacGregors, and I will follow all the rules and won't turn on the T.V.

But it starts with day camp, at six years old.

While Brad writes in "Our Summer Plans" booklet in Mrs. Miller's class that "we know Watervale," I draw a purple stick figure of me holding a fishing pole and write that I am going to a camp that has "real fish." Clearly Mom holds this activity out to me as a carrot. After all, I love throwing ping pong balls into the little goldfish globes at the Children's Fair, so doesn't it follow that I would love to fish?

I never see a pond, or a fishing pole at my day camp that summer, mostly because I am too shy to venture beyond the arts and crafts hut, where I make countless plaster of Paris molds of animals, left to languish on a shelf, or beyond the sides of the above-ground pool where I cling, too scared to take a swimming test. I cry so hard every day the first week that, finally Mom relents, and talks Robbie into taking my place. It is his friends, after all, that are bouncing on the seats in the back of the van that pulls in my driveway every morning to deliver me to this camp.

The next summer is a walk to Brownie day camp every morning, forming lines in the park at the Winnetka Village Green to go to your morning station, be it making lanyards, or clay pots, or going to swimming lessons at the beach. It must have been a rainy summer, because I recall more than one tour of the water filtration plant that summer, the destination being within walking distance with a willing employee there, ready to tour us through the myriad of pipes and holding tanks.

Overnight camp will come too soon for me because I am not a kid who has the confidence to make new friends easily. I, who love to spend Friday nights sleeping at my friends' houses on their bedroom floor, dread my Girl Scout troop camping weekends. There are rules and expectations, and I hate both once I am free from school and household "musts." I watch my sister beg to go to camp for eight weeks. I read her letters she sends home. They are brief notes that say only camp is a blast and she must write this letter as a "ticket" to get into dinner on Sunday.

When I am 11, I am told I am going away to camp. "Camp Douglas Smith," Mom says. "Betsy went there for a year and loved it." It is a camp in Ludington, Michigan; the longtime camp is operated by the village of Winnetka, and Mom assumes that since my older sister attended, and we had lived in Winnetka up until a year ago, I can attend it.

I cannot. That decision places yet another wedge between me, and my friends from Greeley that I had left a year earlier and who will begin a multi-year-relationship with this camp. It means when I visit Sarah in the summer she is singing "Camp CDS we love you" songs and sharing stories with her friends that I am not privy to.

But because camp is a must in our household, I land at a Girl Scout camp that summer, and a Camp Fire Girl camp the next. When I am 13, Mom sends me to High Trails camp in Colorado, where my cousins Cate and Steph have been campers for a few years.

I am scared, insecure and anxious about meeting a whole new group of girls. It is an expensive camp, unlike my previous camps, and the girls who attend come from private schools and big cities. One camper will strum her guitar every evening from her perch on her top bunk and languidly sing "Leavin' on a Jet Plane," bursting into tears halfway through over the pangs of missing her 14-year-old boyfriend at home.

I am unpacking my trunk, the first day. This is a camp where you hang your clothes in a big wooden locker, or place them on the shelves. It is a camp where we sleep on real beds, not cots, and our cabin has a "lounge" with a fireplace and plaid couches.

"Remember kindergarten?" I ask a girl who has just arrived. I am nervously wiping my sweaty palms on my brand-new light blue Wrangler jeans, and I look at Debbie expectantly. She has chosen the locker next to mine, and though the last time I saw Debbie she was a plump four-year-old with curly red hair and saddle shoes, in my junior kindergarten class at Greeley, I recognize her. Now she is a tall, thin 13-year-old with straightened hair.

Debbie glances at me, frowns in concentration, and flips her long red hair over her shoulder. "No," she replies.

I remember.

Debbie is not my friend at camp that summer.

I am determined my own children will like camp; that they will feel they can go away from home with a duffel bag full of clothes knowing they are loved, and missed, and that the new people they meet will want to be their friends. I wait out the three days when my oldest, Kelsey, goes to Girl Scout camp at eight years old, nervously. To me, if it is a bomb—if I sent her at too young an age—I don't know how I will make it up to her. My overzealousness backfires; my daughters love camp, and soon they are pleading with their dad to spend more time at camp than he is comfortable with. I am not sending them away; I am empowering them to know that they can leave home—and Mom and Dad—and make new friends.

When my son Caleb goes to five days of camp, at seven years old, I will tuck his blanket into his sleeping bag in his upper bunk. He will have such a good time that in second grade, during story writing week, he writes such glowing reviews of Camp Abenaki that I give the director color photo copies to use as promotional material.

Maybe I am just someone who has a hard time following rules.

13

CHAPTER TEN
"BAD LEGS"

It is the first lunch hour in sixth grade at Highland Junior High that causes my stomach to cramp and my palms to sweat.

"Who're ya eating with?" I ask Sally. We're locker partners; we grab our paper sacks of lunch from our top locker shelf while clumps of sixth, seventh and eighth graders mill around us.

"My friends," she says. Sally walks away, leaving me to bang the gray metal locker door shut and snap the lock, while she retreats through the school's front doors where we will all eat lunch on the long strip of front lawn.

A dark-haired girl with huge, expressive eyes and a confused look walks by me. "Do you have anyone to eat with?" I ask. We drop down on a square of grass with our paper sacks, sitting cross-legged as best we can in our skirts, and give our tickets to the eighth-grade boy who punches a hole in them and hands us each a small bottle of milk. You eat quickly in junior high, we learn, because the lunch break is mainly about the girls walking around the long, rectangular building—a sort of promenade—while the boys play pick-up sports on the rear playing fields.

My new lunchmate and I begin our journey around the school, but each day, for a week, she ditches me on these walks. So I just keep walking, alone. When did school lunchtime become this deep well of loneliness; this half hour in the middle of the school day that I dread? Greeley School lunch times were a burst out the school doors with my friends, a quick walk down the street home and a bologna sandwich in the backyard or at the kitchen table, and a half hour of playing in my room or back at the school playground. Even in my few months at Riverside, all the girls in my class who stayed at school for lunch sat at the arts and crafts table together.

I get no sympathy at home. "Make new friends," Mom says, but I am slow at this. Can't someone teach me?

I struggle, too, that winter with my changing body.

"She can't go like that." I am in the den, reading a book, waiting on a Sunday afternoon to go to an employee open house at the company where Dad is manager of branches, whatever that means. I can hear Dad in the kitchen. We've been home from church for an hour.

"Like what?" Mom asks, and comes into the den.

I think I am done with all the Rules for the weekend—chores, church—and I am very happy curled up in my blue jeans and T-shirt with a book.

"Go change, Emily," Mom says. "Back into what you wore this morning. We have to leave."

It is a must-do, this open house, and we parade about the factory floor amongst truck parts and displays and industrial equipment, being introduced to nameless people and being told to hold back at the tables of food because Dad is a "host."

I don't even see where Dad has a desk, or makes phone calls. I just want to go home.

One day at school, I tap the shoulder of the girl sitting in front of me in home room and ask her if I can eat lunch with her. Mary becomes my friend. Best of all, my family has joined the First Congregational Church where Mary's family attends, and at long last Sunday School becomes an extension of school—still a place to bear up for an hour—but now at least with kids I know.

On some Fridays, Mary and I shop in downtown Battle Creek with our babysitting money after school and pick out our chocolates at the closet-sized candy shop behind Robinsons' Department Store before her mom picks us up. An hour later we are munching our out-of-a-box-made Chef Boyardee pizza and cutting pictures of Barry Williams of *The Brady Bunch* from Tiger Beat magazine in her basement rec room, waiting for our Friday night line-up of TV shows.

"Should I start another page for him?" This is a big decision because we already have three Barry Williams pages in our big, unwieldy scrapbook of construction paper pages filled with glossy magazine pictures. He does not rate as highly as David Cassidy, who fills nearly the entire book.

Mary laughs and suddenly thrusts a patchwork quilt over the book as her brother comes into the basement rec room. I look up in adulation at this 17-year-old in his wool purple and white letterman's jacket; a large L emblazoned on the front. He has the beginnings of a mustache.

"Oh my God, not again," John rolls his eyes and shuts the door of his basement bedroom. "DON'T go in my bedroom," he adds as he takes the stairs two at a time, ridding himself of 13-year-old girls.

"Watch the bumps," I say as Mary smears Elmer's glue on the flip side of Barry's head. We decide not to start a new page; there is room for one more smiling shot of Barry holding a basketball which I paste next to Mitch Vogel. Mary does not want a whole page for Mitch. I am the one in love with this red-haired adolescent who plays the unwanted orphan on Bonanza; I am the one whose heart constricts while I watch him from the shag carpeting in our basement rec room, on TV on Sunday nights, with his puppy-dog look at the camera when Ben tells him to be loved, he must first love.

Once we move to Battle Creek, we don't eat meals together on weekends, except for lunch and dinner on Sunday. Really, I didn't talk to Dad. In Battle Creek, he disappeared early Monday mornings and reappeared after dinner Thursday.

Like "Bonanza's" Ben Carson, Mary's father is kind, with big, soulful eyes and a ready grin. He owns a heating company, and comes to our house to install a stove in our basement and comes to clean it every fall. He is friendly and talks to me. I go on a weekend visit to their cabin, and I wonder what it's like to have a dad who is so kind.

In our 1967 Christmas card photo, I stand stiffly in a lime green dress, with knee socks, next to Rob. My brother exudes eighth-grade confidence; he is a very good-looking teenage boy, and Betsy smiles. My eyes seem to penetrate the camera, searching for acceptance from someone. My dress is too short; I know because Shannon, from next door and in seventh grade, told me after school. "Blue and green looks good on you, Emily," her mom says when she overhears us.

My dress is too short.

•——◆

"Dirty," Gina laughs at her response to Mrs. White, the gym teacher, during third period on Mondays. We are lined up in the girls' gym, a smaller sized version of the boys gym downstairs, and during roll call must tell our red-haired teacher, in her white shorts, white blouse, and white Keds, if our gym suits are clean or dirty.

Our grade is based, in part, on whether we take our blue cotton one-piece gym suits home every Friday to be washed before Monday. She makes a check mark before we start our jumping jacks, just as she will stand outside the communal shower in the locker room and mark in a little box in her grade book whether we shower.

The B-on my report cards for phys. ed reflects the fact that, while I wash my gym suit weekly and shower, I do not join the Girls Athletic Association or show any inkling of coordination in square dancing, interpretive dance or basketball.

Mom, also, refuses to buy me a new gym suit, and I must wear Betsy's hand-me-down, which is not wrinkle free Dacron like the other girls. "You can just wear Betsy's," she says. "It's a waste of money to get a new one." Betsy's old gym suit also has her name, not mine, above the chest pocket. If I iron it on Sunday evenings, I will get an A for appearance but mostly it is wrinkled, and very baggy on me. Embroidered names in back and front are required, and I so envy the girls with their name stitched by machine from the local uniform supplier.

In junior high, I feel that if I make the seventh-grade cheerleading squad, the boys will like me and Dad will think I am good at something. Right now, all I can do is play the flute. I am first chair, but that is because Mom wants me to have private lessons.

I don't know if Dad knows I am good at that. Usually, the concerts are on a Wednesday evening and Dad is always out of town.

"I gotta make cheerleading," I tell Mary in the spring. "Then I'm pretty sure I can get a boyfriend."

I have already failed month-long charm school at Robinson's department store and am not chosen to be a weekend model as my next-door neighbor Shannon is. Her older sister and I try, on the Saturday tryout session, but we both perspire miserably as we change from wool kilts to polyester pants suits and vinyl-looks-like-leather jumpers, and fail to smile as we try to walk like a model through the two-story department store,

If I am a cheerleader, I will get to wear the blue and gold cotton twirly skirt to school on game days. I will wear suspenders under the blue V-neck sweater to hold up the skirt, like all the cheerleaders do, and my sweater will have three big gold chenille letters, HJH, sewn at an angle down the front and I will get to act very cool.

"Again," Shannon says to me in my living room where we are chanting "United we stand, divided we fall, Mighty

Hawks conquer all!" over and over, with sprawling jumps and hops and placing our arms in a V. "This time smile, Emily," Shannon says. "You gotta show you're having fun!" I stare out into the frozen expanse of our yard and hope that I will be good enough, because if I am, everything will change. I will have a boyfriend and hold his hand in the hallway when Mr. Fritz isn't looking. He will hang out at my locker until the bus comes and maybe he will sneak to Roy's store and buy bubble gum for me. I don't know any girls who sneak to Roy's, only boys, and none of them ever buy gum for me, except Rob, when I give him the money and practically beg him.

Tryouts are in the girls' gym, after school. We change into our gym suits in the basement locker room, and troop up the stairs. On the bleachers sit Mrs. White, and the eight, eighth-grade cheerleaders who will all decide on the upcoming seventh and eighth-grade squads. I am in the middle of the line of girls waiting to try out, in groups of six, chanting our United We Stand cheer. The simple arm and leg movements are embedded in my brain, as are the words; my heart is pounding as I stand in baggy uniform and go through the motions.

I clutch library books under my arm the next morning as I squeeze through the throng of girls anxious to look at the list of next year's cheerleaders posted, ironically, outside the counseling office. Some fifty girls mob the hallway, clutching books against their breasts for their first period class, and the sweaty. nervous mass shifts as each girl looks up at the list to see if there is a red "yes" next to her name.

Perspiration darkens my armpits; I am about to find out if I will have a good life for the next two years, or simply exist.

I do not make the cheerleading squad.
I am, I decide, a failure.

> "Well you know June, when you come right down to it, sometimes it's pretty tough being a kid,"
>
> Ward to June, "Next Door Indians," season 1, episode 28.

Would my years as a not-comfortable-in-my-own-body teenager have been made easier had I made that cut in the spring of 1968 and had been issued a cotton cheerleader skirt? Would my ease with 13-year-old boys have soared, had I been able to stand in front of my locker wearing the blue HJH sweater, blue knee socks, and white sneakers, and twirled the skirt as I turned to laugh at a joke?

When my oldest daughter doesn't make the seventh-grade cuts for cheerleading at Essex Middle School, in 2004, I feel, momentarily, a stab of loss. It is very brief, and Kelsey takes the cut in stride; she is busy already with soccer and track. "It doesn't matter, Mom," she says. "In high school you can't do other sports if you're a cheerleader. I probably wouldn't have stuck with it."

By eighth grade, I am no longer actually *in* science or math; I am somewhere else in my head. A library book fits nicely within my moss-green eighth grade Algebra textbook, and kind Mrs. Doman cannot see me as I read in the back row. I am anywhere but in this classroom, where numbers are being taught.

In eighth-grade science where there is no heavy textbook, I simply disappear in my head. Mostly I replay scenes from "To Kill a Mockingbird." While I have yet to read the book, the movie awakens in me that both women, and people of color, are not treated fairly, and I cannot seem to accept those injustices. I love the library at Highland Junior High, and spend many happy hours in the stacks of the room tucked away on the second floor, discovering an author, Lenora Mattingly Weber, who will write of a fictional motherless family whose father loves them endlessly.

My own father travels for business all week long and returns home to play golf and go to parties on the weekends. Mom does show him my report cards. One Thursday evening he returns home from a business trip with a small, hand-held gadget that is designed to help with math basics. He hands it to me.

I put it in a desk drawer.

"You won't really need much math later on," says Mom, herself a math major in college. "You know, your dad flunked calculus in college and he's done fine. "Don't worry about it."

I do worry. I do very poorly on my math SAT's; I am lucky enough to go to a college that doesn't require any math, and I struggle mightily after college as a newspaper reporter trying to understand budgets.

You need math.

I just want Dad to care that I don't get math. I want him to know who my friends are, and that I need to know he loves me.

He doesn't, so I read my books and write in my diary about the teachers I have crushes on,

"He's pretty mean, isn't he?'" Tory says to me. We are on her double bed, sharing stories about which teachers are the cutest at Highland. Our note-passing at school goes well until Mr. Pitts intercepts a note one day while he's lecturing us on Earth Day. We have just come from lunch. It is hot-lunch day, and we licked the sugary glaze of doughnuts off our fingers after our thirty-five-cent lunch of a sloppy joe and potato chips and doughnut. I sit, frozen, at the long table I share with another student, as Mr. Pitts opens the notebook paper folded into a tiny little square. He is a very young teacher—probably right out of college—and his face reddens as he reads a line or two. He crumples the note, and tosses it in the basket. "We won't talk about this," he says. Clearly, college ed classes hadn't prepared him for the crushes of his 13-year-old students.

It is the beginning of my boy crazy years and I don't remember having Dad in my life, at all. Did we argue? Was he anything to me those years other than the man in the house who has to be kept happy? The man who never talks.

Why can't he tell me that I am a cherished, beautiful young girl who he loves, simply because he chose to have children? I keep trying to earn his love, by playing in the band, trying out for cheerleading, going to church and making cookies for him on the weekends.

But there is so little response.

I am a late bloomer. When I am 13, I go to see "Summer of '42" and I am absolutely convinced that a boy would never touch a girl's breasts, despite the groping I see on the screen. What would be the reason? A year later I am lying on the top bunk in my best friend Peggy's bedroom and we are talking, in this very non threatening way in which we can't see each other, about how to kiss a boy.

"I don't get it," I say. "Do you just smash your lips together?" It is a Friday night, and in this small bedroom on Moorland Drive in Battle Creek, Peggy and I ponder what it would be like to have boyfriends. I am both scared and thrilled at the prospect, and in some ways, I want nothing more than to walk out of the football stadium bleachers, en masse with the LHS Spartans marching band in which I contribute minimally as a flute player, hand-in-hand with a boyfriend.

In the privacy of my neighbor's family room, late on Saturday evenings after I have put my babysitting charge in bed, I sit inches away from the television screen and watch two adults kissing, wondering how it works. I am yearning for an instruction book—just as I will peruse bookstores in the 1980s, looking for a "how-to" book on falling in love. Dad is, I imagine, confused by me. At 16 years old, I write the names of whatever boy I am dying to date across the binding of my vinyl-covered diary, and now it is a rainbow of faded colors of Mike, Don, Rick, Jeff, Stan... My crushes rarely result in anything so each time my source of affection changes, I choose a bolder pen color to obliterate the last boy's name. Any time with Dad is spent playing sports, but there is such a competition between me and Rob for attention from Dad, that family activities are filled with arguments.

The night before my first day at Lakeview High School, I am so gut-wrenchingly nervous that I consider throwing myself down the plant-covered, mossy bank from our stone patio to our waterfront on Goguac Lake. I will tell Mom I slipped, and with any luck I will break an arm or leg before tumbling onto the small rocks along the shoreline.

This would buy me a day's delay in walking into the sprawling one-story high school with its labyrinth of hallways and hundreds of teenagers all of whom, I'm convinced, are far more secure than I am.

"Did you ask Rob when the bus leaves?" Mom returns me to what is staring me in the face: dinner dishes and a new bus schedule. My plan of refuge is quickly dismissed as I do, once again, just what Mom asks. It's the "can-do" mode, the old go-forward, don't-think-about-it, feelings-don't-count mentality that's allowed me to put one foot in front of the other for the past thirteen years.

"A little after seven, I think," Rob says an hour later, not looking up from the motorcycle engine he is taking apart on the gravel spur of our driveway. He lifts a greasy hand and uses the back of it to brush away his bangs. "I'm getting a ride, so I'm not sure. Just be at the bus stop at seven."

He is dismissing me—his little sister—but I stand there with my paper schedule in hand. He looks up at me with his brown eyes. They are large, soft and expressive and in his last two years of high school he will win and reject many girlfriends. "Rob, I have split lunch," I say, studying my class schedule as if memorizing it will help me navigate the maze of hallways the next day.

"Lemme see," he takes the paper with the two grease-free fingers of his left hand and reads it.

"Yeah... you gotta get all the way from one end of the building down to the cafeteria and you got a short lunch. You gottta run or the line will be too long. That's gross," He hands me back the crinkled paper, now marked by two spots of grease, and works on loosening a bolt.

"It's rough," he says as I turn to walk back to the house.

I take this nugget of interest, and comfort, from my older brother and hope it will sustain me through the next day. But I just know that I will not know how to find my classes and, of course, I will have no one to eat lunch with and everyone walking through the cafeteria will most assuredly see that I am sitting alone adrift among the eight-seater rectangular tables. I am not a lunch person. It is an undefined meal; one in which if you eat too much or take too much time from your day you feel sluggish, and if you eat too little or skip it you lack energy. Since my eat-at-home days of elementary school when Mom placed my bologna or peanut butter sandwich on the table, with a glass of milk, an apple and two cookies, lunch has always kind of confused me.

I nestle into my bed, an hour later, and slide open the small white cabinet door of my bookshelf headboard. I grasp the familiar softness of my vinyl diary; it is bright, shiny maroon and the front cover is padded, so that when I clutch it each night before going to sleep, the same warm feeling bubbles in my stomach that I had all the years I clutched a soft, stuffed Koala bear next to my cheek.

The tiny brass key to this diary is hidden between the pages of a book, also near my pillow in the bookshelf headboard, and I take the key and slide the little tumblers open. It is a ritual I have practiced every night since Gram gifted me this diary at Christmas. Did my always-happy, unconditionally-loving grandmother know I would make this palm-sized book a constant in my life for the next five years? Did Gram, who will suffer desperately from Alzheimer's disease the last ten years of her life, know that this simple book of cardboard, vinyl, paper pages and paste, will still be next to my bed fifty years later?

I choose from my rainbow array of felt tip pens, and jot in aqua on this night before my first day of high school that I am scared and wishing my best friend, Peggy, is in more of my classes. I write that I am praying I will get through the day. I am sincere.

I will write on the six lines allotted for the daily entry, nearly every day for five years, until I've finished the first semester of my freshman year in college, and also fill in the blank pages with self-improvement resolutions—losing weight, clearing up my acne and suspending my worrying. Now, I hold the puffy vinyl cover up to my cheeks and it feels cool and comforting and simply reinforces that knowing my feelings so well is both a blessing and a curse.

"They sell Coke and M & M's in the snack bar," Sally says the next day as she and I sit in the sweltering cafeteria with a few other girls from our English class. This class is split in half, with a seventeen-minute lunch break, and to my relief I find that we all just rush down the hallways to stand at the back of the lunch line. Moms volunteering in white aprons and standing behind the steam trays plop goulash and white bread on our aqua Melamine trays and we choose from chocolate or butterscotch pudding, a little blob of whipped cream wilting in the late August heat. Sally and I tumble into seats at a table of two other girls from our class. It is so noisy and hot that we want to pull off our panty hose.

"The football guys sell the candy," Sally says. She stands up to dump her tray of its contents and waits to see who will follow. But I eat my squishy white bread and goulash while others dump their meals and stand in line for the candy. I will not be as carefree in high school as these girls are.

In early September evenings the high school marching band practices the prancing and formations on the high school parking lot with our teacher Mr. Moore, perched atop a cherry picker, of sorts, so he can direct seventy-five teenagers as they march about on asphalt. Our attention spans are short on these mellow late-summer evenings, and when he tires of yelling at us through his megaphone, he calls a break. "Ten minutes," Mr. Moore says, one hand clutching at his short beard in anxiety, "and be right back in your spot. Go to the bathroom—do what you have to do—but be ready!" Peggy and I tuck our flutes under our arms and wander off to the grass to fall in a heap. It seems nearly every other girl links hands with her boyfriends. Sally intertwines her fingers with Jeff, and they laugh. She is still wearing the purple and white skirt and purple sweater of the JV cheerleaders, having come to band practice straight from a game. A little part of me cries inside.

When I do finally have a crack at a relationship with a good-looking swim team guy, I blow it.

"I just, ya know, came over to see you," Mike says, standing outside our front door on an October Saturday evening. I am a junior at LHS. I am home alone. Never are Mom and Dad home on a Saturday night unless our house is filled with their friends. Because of this, I will be nearly sixty years old before I feel comfortable simply enjoying a quiet evening at home on a Saturday.

We play pool at the neighbors where I have a standing invitation because I am their steady babysitter. "Mike talked to me in the hallway," I pen in my diary on October 10, 1972, and place a "marvelous day" sticker with a smiley face on the page. One month later I write that "I have lost him." After the first swim meet of the season on a Friday evening, I rush to the cafeteria with the other girls dating boys on the team. But his girlfriend, already in college, has returned home for the weekend and he is grinning widely, his swim bag in one hand and her hand in his other

I feel I am a social flop and I want Dad to tell me I am smart, beautiful, and worthy of his love. I do not wear makeup, like Shannon next door, and I do not know how to tease the boys on the bus, and I do not make the cuts for the synchronized swim team or for Flag Girls.

For both, you need long, shapely legs. Mine are short and stubby.

Gail, a classmate, is also short. But she is a cheerleader at Highland, a Pom Pom girl and in Aqua Sprites at Lakeview, and she has lots of boyfriends.

"He calls them hotdogs," Gail says at tennis practice after school. Gail flips her long brown hair and flashes her huge smile, and her eyes light up at the mention of her dad. We are the beneficiaries of Title IX, the federal education law passed a few months earlier, requiring, among other things, girls' access to school sports, and our team of ten girls is brand new. I make a low-level spot on the team. Gail, whose eyes light up at the mention of her physician dad, says, "He said at breakfast, 'Ann, does Gail have any 'hotdog' sweats for tennis practice? It's getting cold in the afternoons. If not, I'll stop at Jack Pearl's and pick some up today.' But Mom said that she found out where to buy warm-up suits, for girls, in Kalamazoo, so she told dad she's getting me one."

Her dad cares.

"He bought me a new pair of Blue Tips on Saturday," Gail adds, not exactly bragging but clearly enjoying talking about her dad in front of me and the rest of the tennis team. "When we went into the shoe store he said, 'Do you have any little boy sizes for my 16-year-old daughter? She's got little feet.'"

Did Dad not care or did my mother just not let him care? The irony in my tennis-team relationship with Gail is that we were naturals to be friends.

I will be in college before I kiss a boy.

It is not until May of 1974, just a month before graduation, that my traveling father rescues me and improves my social standing simply by doing what he had done for the past seven years—travel. He buys an apple green Ford Mustang convertible, and I am able to drop him at W.K. Kellogg Regional Airport on Monday mornings and drive his car until he returns Thursday evenings. Hence my ability to drive students to the A & W for lunch every day, and sit on the back of the car with the top down munching chili dogs and greasy onion rings, which inches me up in the popularity poll.

I do not understand, then, that a confident smile goes a long way in life. I believe my Dad is too busy confidently smiling at his forklift customers all over the map to explain that to me.

"Shut your eyes and put out your arms," Ralph tells me minutes after I've dumped my sleeping bag and duffel in a corner of the hospitality room at the First Congregational Church in Battle Creek. I am 15 and Mom has convinced me to attend a weekend youth retreat. "Just walk around and feel people and ask questions and decide who they are." There are about sixteen of us in this rectangular room, and Ralph, the youth minister, and a parent, are standing sentinel to make sure we don't bump into furniture or touch the wrong body parts. I stumble up to a body and thrust hands forward, feeling the softness of a flannel shirt. "Jim?" I guess, trying to think of the boys in my youth group. He laughs, and all of a sudden, I know I'm going to be OK. The next day we walk three blocks through the February winds to the Haven of Rest Rescue Mission in Battle Creek. Black men in winter parkas worn shiny, and torn work pants, hang outside the front door with cigarettes dangling from their lips. We attend the five p.m. service required before eating the 6 p.m. dinner, and I have more questions than can be answered.

The Haven of Rest rescue Mission in Battle Creek is close to the monolithic First Congregational Church, and it is during the weekend youth retreat that I become aware of the solitary brick building with adult men loitering outside its doors. I remember thinking that my exposure to minorities hadn't improved since leaving Winnetka. I wonder why, and how, my family can have so much yet, in my opinion, Dad shares so little of himself with me, and people who are poor. What is Dad holding on to?

I am tongue-tied around almost all boys and men—except for my grandfathers—but my relationship with Ralph, who is probably 30, is a comfortable one. He is my friend under the guise of God's love, so it feels OK to me. I feel like he accepts me, and in fact, I think he does, as youth minister, and brings us emotionally together away from the social expectations of high school.

I don't feel this unconditional acceptance from Dad.

The french-cut green beans crunched so loudly I can hear Dad's chewing all the way in the kitchen.

I get up from the counter where I am doing Latin

homework, and take a slender, dark green bean out of the saucepan. I bite down on it; the bean is cold, and very crunchy. I look in the pan and see little shards of ice on the remaining beans.

"Guess I didn't cook the beans long enough," I say to Dad. It is eight p.m. on a Thursday. He is sitting in his green recliner, next to the sliding glass door in the den with a view of the lake, and is eating his dinner of baked potato, baked chicken and green beans at a TV table. His tie is loosened, but he is still wearing a dark pin-striped suit and black oxfords. Mom is away on one of her rare solo trips. My instructions from her were to have his dinner ready by eight when he'd arrive home from out of town.

Dad looks up from the newspaper on his lap. "No... no they're fine," he says. "Thanks for dinner."

"Dad, I think they're still frozen. Want me to cook 'em longer?"

I stand at the entrance to the den. I am nervous. "Guess I never cooked beans before."

"They're good Emily. Just kinda crunchy." Dad smiles a little.

I retreat to the kitchen and my Latin translation.

That night, I cry myself to sleep. I am 16, and I can't even talk to my dad about green beans.

REPORT CARD F-1970-71 THEODORE THOMAS

LAKEVIEW HIGH 9652201

STUDENT LAST NAME	FIRST NAME	SEX	GRADE
THAYER	EMILY	F	09

SUBJECT	CREDIT	TEACHER	FIRST PERIOD MARK	C		AB	SECOND PERIOD MARK	C		AB
CITIZENSHIP	.50	PHILLIPS	B+	1		02	B-	1		01
BAND RESERVE	.50	MOORE	A	1	M	00	A	1	M	00
ALG I R	.50	FELTON	C	2	R	01	C	2		01
ENGLISH I R	.50	DEWAARD	B+	1	M	02	A-	1	M	01
LATIN I	.50	FITZGERALD	B	2	R	02	B	2	R	03
PHY ED I GIRLS	.50	PHY ED STAFF	B-	1	J	0	B	2		03

CHAPTER ELEVEN
"REVIVAL"

Foam spills over the plastic cup as I watch him hand the beer to the boy with long hair and a lazy grin. This boy, in turn, thrusts the foamy cup into my hand as I step into the fraternity house; a steady stream of freshmen pushing me forward. I am amazed at this first boy's sleight-of-hand, pumping the keg and releasing a steady stream of beer into the cups, all the while checking the "new meat" at Ohio Wesleyan University, where I am a freshman.

If I can find the bathroom and dump most of this beer, I think I can hold the nearly empty cup and fake feeling drunk.

It is an early September evening, 1974, and I have never held a cup of keg beer before, nor beer in a bottle or can, other than to pass a chilled can of Stroh's to Dad at the outlet at Watervale. On the night of high school graduation, my friend Peggy and I make the rounds of parties; it is the end of high school, and I no longer care if I am really invited to these gatherings. I don't drink; I am turned off by classmates "barfing" on front lawns—or so I write in my diary—and by midnight I go home, not even trying to shed high school insecurities and simply hang out with my peers.

In college, I want only to fit in; to make friends and be separate from my parents. Ohio Wesleyan is not my first choice.

I'd been determined to major in journalism at Northwestern University and return to my comfortable stomping grounds, the suburbs of Chicago, but I'm rejected by that school, I'm sure in no small part due to my embarrassingly-low math SAT scores. It is God's intervention that leads me to Ohio Wesleyan. Refusing any advice from my mom about "creating options" for myself and applying to less selective colleges, I mention one day to my high school journalism teacher/church youth group adviser that Northwestern is my one and only choice.

"I think you oughta look at Ohio Wesleyan," Dick, a 1969 OWU graduate, says. I am in the back seat of his 1970 Ford Pinto on a Sunday afternoon, headed to the Columbia Avenue Burger Chef where our youth group always ends our meetings. His casual, off-hand suggestion is a good one.

The Admissions Department at Ohio Wesleyan sees beyond my low math scores and admits me. My four years there are nearly all positive. It feels right from the moment I meet my roommate and, within the first hour, my longtime friend, Amy.

I also click well with the late Verne Edwards, the Journalism Department chairman. He assumes a paternal/mentor role for many of us and I find in him incredible dedication to churning out quality journalists as well as to the father role I feel I am lacking. He was, I realize now, the "Martie Malone" of my junior-high *Beany Malone* books, a kind, earnest, newspaper-loving father who forgave mistakes. I revered him, as did so many others, as evidenced by the return of so many of his former students for his memorial service in 2014.

Is it luck, or "enterprise" on my part (the phrase used on the *Gilson Wight Award for Journalistic Enterprise* certificate

I receive at graduation) that one afternoon I overhear Professor Edwards on the phone with the editor of the *Fostoria Review-Times,* a small daily newspaper in northwest Ohio. It is the winter of my senior year. The editor is seeking a paid intern for ten weeks that spring. I interview and am hired.

My editor in Fostoria, I soon learn, has two passions: the slices of butterscotch, chocolate cream and lemon meringue pies under the glass-topped domes on the counter at the diner where we eat lunch every day, and, to my great benefit, a goal of seeking out the unusual in this town of 15,000 people, for newspaper coverage.

On a Sunday evening, the newspaper's photographer Stan, and I, are sent to a small, tucked-away church to cover a revival. I have, essentially, no faith in my life, not connecting the dots of my previous good fortune to any spirituality.

"Gonna be a hoot," Stan says as we climb the stairs to the wooden church building.

Stan is tall, young, with a bushy blond mustache and is fun. Like other young photographers I will work with for a few years, he readily challenges the editor and pushes boundaries.

His camera hangs from his neck and I clutch a notebook. I smile weakly. "Yeah," I say.

"We're here to say something to the glory of God this evening," the Reverend Toy-Mary Grant, in a white robe with long dark hair cascading down her back, tells the people scattered in the wooden pews. A visiting Evangelist preacher, Reverend Sam Barber, is visiting this chosen place, the Light House of Holiness Church in Fostoria, Ohio, she says, because God has led him here.

Was I open-minded toward this holy roller service? I doubt not. Stan and I laugh for days, asking each other in the second story newsroom if we were "saved." I cover the story with awe and disbelief.

Dancing, hopping, shaking and speaking in tongues, I write in the article in the Review-Times on April 25, 1978, the people attending the service "reach a plateau," Rev. Barber said.

"God has seen this place," Rev. Toy-Grant declares at the service's closure. "God has been here and will never leave you."

It is an evening that stays with me forever. Though I've not spoken in tongues, nor even attended a similar revival service, I don't doubt the power of God.

"It's better," the blond, tousle-haired salesman says, "than anything else on the lot."

Roger, the lanky young man who had greeted us twenty minutes earlier at the door of the Pontiac dealership, grins so widely that his eyes almost crinkle shut. "Let's taker 'er out," he says and puts a hand on my shoulder as he steers me toward the bright red Karmann Ghia, a low-slung car only half the bulk of its neighboring Firebirds and Pintos.

I glance at Dad for approval. Cars are a man's territory. Dad stands in the late-afternoon September sunshine with his suit jacket slung over his right shoulder and his striped tie loosened. "Try it," he nods. "But it's not practical."

> "I've gotta get my father's permission to buy it," Wally to a friend. "Well, I feel for you kid. I know what I went through to get my father's permission."
>
> "Wally Buys a Car," season 6, episode 16.

This is my first car purchase, made quickly because I had decided the night before that I can't return to college without a car. I'm entering my junior year.

Roger steers the little car off the lot and glances over at me. "College?" he asks, and I nod. "This'll be great for road trips. Cheap on gas." He pulls over and trades seats with me, brushing shaggy blond bangs out of his eyes, and directs me onto Capital Avenue.

"Just let 'er go," Roger rolls down his window and motions his right hand forward as if propelling me to a higher speed. "Wish I'd had a car like this when I was 19. Course I wish I'd gone to college too. Maybe I wouldn't have gone to Vietnam then. Two years."

"Was it as bad as people say?" I ask, glancing over at this good looking 20-something-year-old and already wondering how I'd convince Dad this Karmann Ghia is my car.

"You don't wanna know. Do I wish I'd gone to college instead? Yeah. Did I get stoned every night over there? If I could. I got messed up. Hey, take a right and you can get your speed up on the penetrator." Roger sticks a tanned arm out the window and points to a freeway entrance. "But it did get me away from my high school girlfriend. She was the homecoming queen at Battle Creek Central, and everyone thought we'd get married."

"So where are you in college?" Roger's knee brushes against mine as he twists to look out the tiny rear window. "Man, that guy's tailgating us. Ya gotta be careful driving these small cars. Some of these truckers try to push you off the road."

"In Ohio," I say. "I'm not around here much. My parents are pretty much 'my way or the highway,' so I just avoid coming home."

Roger has those blue eyes that just go with blond hair, and when he flashes me a sympathetic glance, I try to pretend he understands my relationship with Mom and Dad, but really, I know he is just trying to sell me a car. I know all about monthly commissions and quotas because Dad talks about them all the time.

But I want this car. I want it so badly I feel like my thighs have melted into the sticky, hot vinyl of the front seat and my hands are molded onto the black steering wheel. I clutch it tighter and reach down to shift to a higher gear. Do I want this car because Roger-who-went-to-Vietnam and has cool hair and dated a homecoming queen is the salesman? Or do I want it because it is little and red and fun to drive? Or because I know Dad will say it's impractical, and that makes me happy. Very happy.

"Common sense," Mom used to say to us, "is a really important quality. Your dad and I have common sense. That's why you have bedtimes, duties to do on Saturdays and you take swimming lessons. It's just good common sense."

This is why I am boring, didn't have a good boyfriend in high school and hadn't even drunk a beer before I went to college. Too much good ol' common sense.

I just want to be a fun person.

•——◆

"Oh, my God!" Nancy and Suzy and Sandy jump up and screech when they find out they're on the homecoming court. It is at the end of sixth period in high school—American Government—when Mr. Thomas announces via intercom, "Your senior class homecoming court for the class of 1974!" Ten senior girls are named every year and it is the coolest award you can get at Lakeview High School.

"Every day next week our ten homecoming court members will be dressed in the same colors, so look for them and get to know them because on Friday you will vote for your queen," Mr. Thomas continues in his booming voice.

The "triplet" cheerleaders in my class are still smiling and kind of bouncing and acting surprised, when really, we all could have named the homecoming court by our second week of school our freshman year. The ultra-popular rise to the top pretty quickly in high school and usually hold that spot until about a month before graduation. Then all bets are off.

When you spend most of your four years in high school wishing you wore a purple cheerleading skirt and yearning for a popular boy to hold hands with, you carry emotional baggage. I carry it like an albatross when I am 21; when I am in my 60s, I don't know whether to chide myself—or laugh—for clicking on random Facebook pages of the most popular people I knew 45 years ago, just to see how they have aged.

So yeah, in 1977, I want to buy the red car from Roger who'd dated the homecoming queen. I want to pretend Roger likes me.

"You should take this next exit," Roger says. "We can take

the frontage road back and you can see how she feels without those trucks on the road. She's great, isn't she?" he adds, and I look over to see if he's smiling at me. He is, of course. He is a salesman and they always smile. I notice how the dark black of his wristwatch band sets off the tan of his forearm. "You think 'Dad' will like it?"

"My dad works at Clark. He sells forklifts and he wants me to buy American," I say. "But he likes Volkswagens. Mostly he just has to help me find a car pretty quickly so I can leave for college. So, I dunno."

Dad's and my drive home is quiet. Dad doesn't argue. I guess he just doesn't know how to. When we—Betsy and Rob and I—are young and want to try to change Dad's mind, we never talk to him, we just go right to Mom. If she tries to get him to change his mind, he doesn't say anything except maybe "OK," or "no, that doesn't work." That is all. Mom argues with Rob. A lot.

So, I don't know how to argue with Dad about how badly I want to buy the red Karmann Ghia. I will never, in a million years, tell him I will feel as popular as the homecoming queen if I buy the car. Never.

"It's a cool car, Dad," I say as we drive the 15 minutes home on a sticky September evening.

"Not very safe," Dad says, his left, deeply-tanned elbow and forearm resting on the open drivers' side window and his brow furrowing ever so slightly. He doesn't take his eyes off the road. Dad is a very safe driver. "You should go back and look at the Datsun, next to it, tomorrow. It's bigger. It's Japanese, but I guess you need to find a car."

Dad tells me he wants me to buy a used car from this

particular dealer because they buy his forklift trucks. All my life we have tried to only buy stuff where Dad sells trucks. I couldn't have a Schwinn bike until I am 10, when Dad finally sold the local Schwinn dealer a forklift truck. My first bike, at seven, was a Hercules Roadmaster.

As we pull into our curving driveway, I know I will spend the one thousand dollars I have saved only on a car Dad approves of. I must please him.

When the phone rings after dinner, I practically run into the kitchen and grab the avocado green receiver off the telephone nestled on the table. "Want to come in tomorrow and seal the deal?" Roger asks, and I can hear the grin in his voice. I, of course, had told him earlier I only had two days to make the car purchase before returning to school. I also had added that college is not where I wanted to be, and that my parents did not know who I was. At all.

"It'll be hard to find a repair shop, you can't take any passengers in the backseat and the odometer's turned over so we have no idea of the mileage on the car," Dad says. He is relaxing in a webbed patio chair, his feet on a low table. Roger is waiting on the phone to hear my answer. Dad lowers the Enquirer and News to his lap. "Buy the other car we saw first, the Datsun. It's not really what I'd buy but you don't have any more time."

I glance at the low orb of an orange sun setting over the lake, and I wonder if I can get Mom to convince him the red car is the one for me. But he has picked up the paper again. He is done talking. "Tell the salesman you'll be back in the morning to drive the Datsun again. I can meet you there at lunchtime."

We live on a lake, with a motorboat, sailboat and canoe moored just below our patio. One block away is a country club, with a golf course and tennis courts, where my parents hang out on weekends.

I have been home exactly twenty-four hours and I cannot wait to leave.

Six years later I will write a light-hearted Father's Day column for a weekly newspaper I am working for, the *Wilmette News*. "I forgive you Dad," I write, "for telling me not to buy a car I really wanted. You were protecting me."

At least I am *trying* to understand the choke Dad has on me at age 26 when I write that column. But I don't loosen that chokehold for a long time. I gotta go through a lot of Rogers, first.

In college, I ask Don out on a date my junior year, because my roommate Jennie asks me, "What are you waiting for?"

He is different from all the other guys I date. He is husky, has a receding hairline at 21 years old, is distanced from his father who has spent years as a missionary in Vietnam, and tentative. There is an attraction, and had we played out a college romance and let it go at his graduation at the end of my junior year, I could reflect on a good time. An uncomplicated time. But Don, an art major and I, a writer who is channeling my passion into journalism, mutually fuel the attraction and hang on for a long time.

Don is the first boy to kiss me where I feel excitement bubble up inside of me, and I stare into a mirror that night in my dorm room to try to really see the *new* me.

While both enjoying and suffering the up-and-down young-love pangs for six months, we become incredibly close the following summer, most likely heightened by distance and mutual frustration with our jobs. Our relationship unfolds in letters. I am working in the kitchen of a dude ranch in Big Timber, Montana, waitressing in a rigorously -controlled environment. Don is in California at a similarly lowly job.

Sadly, I am miserable in a beautiful place because I miss him so much.

I arrive in Big Timber, Montana in mid-June, 1977, shortly before midnight, on a Greyhound bus. There is no one to meet me, and I wander into the one open business in this small town, and check into the hotel. I call my boss at the Lazy K, a sprawling dude ranch some thirty miles outside of town, and she tells me the letter of my arrival had not been received. Her son, Tack, will be in town by noon the next day to pick me up. I pay my seven dollar tab the next morning, and sit on a park bench writing a long, lonely letter to Don. Tack arrives, as promised, and as we head to the Lazy K that afternoon, the bed of his pick-up filled with supplies, I feel a wave of panic. While the ranch is beautiful, nestled at the foothills of the Crazy Mountains, it is far from any town and more remote than I could possibly imagine. I share a platform tent for the summer, with Barb, and rise at six a.m. to clean the lodge along with my three fellow waitresses, and then serve three meals. We hike on our occasional days off, take trail rides when the guest list is short. I chafe at the no-drinking, no-leaving-the-ranch rules.

"I need to be with you," Don's frequent letters inevitably

say. I run to a quiet spot on the brook after I can leave the kitchen in the evening, and devour his letters, and those from my grandfather, with whom I have started a letter-writing relationship. Baba, too, is lonely in his retirement townhouse, with my grandmother spending more and more time in the hospital. I gloss over Baba's letters, cheered that he is thinking of me, but obsess over Don's, and by mid-August, I invite him to come to Montana. I quit my job a week early when he arrives.

The back of the flatbed trucks that Don and I ride in, in late August after he arrives at the ranch, are generally dirty and provide a bumpy ride, but we sit next to each other, our backpacks propped against the rear and we are happy. I am happy. We are hitchhiking to Glacier National Park, where my friend Amy is working. We will eat bologna for a week; I don't recall why. I have money, but Don, graduated, and now without a job and aware of student loans coming due, is on a tight budget. I love the feeling of being poor with him; of his needing me.

I won't be able to walk away from that need for five more years. And when I do, some very little part of me—tiny but wonderful nonetheless—is lost one November day, in 1982.

"It's over," I say. It is a Wednesday evening, after nine p.m. when long distance rates go down, and I scrunch into a corner of the couch in my tiny Evanston living room. I'm on the phone with Don, who is the recipient of my break-up letter.

I'd come to work Monday morning showing my co-worker an envelope. "It's the last letter I'm going to write explaining why we can't keep going," I say to Blair. She is 15 years older than me, married with two children. She lifts her glasses and looks directly at me. "Then *make* it the last one," she says, and returns to tapping out a restaurant review on her computer.

My Aunt Ginny has told me for three years that I am being unfair to Don, that she thinks he loves me more than I do him, and it's not fair of me to hang on. But Don is everything Dad is not—artistic and kind– and very willing to say he loves me. I look at my co-worker Blair, and finally I see something I want, a marriage, children, a career and a home she loves. I am very scared that I won't have my *Leave it-to-Beaver* life with Don because he is so very passionate about his art. And he is poor. He is in grad school.

I am too scared—too spoiled perhaps—to risk ignoring my practical self and pay attention to my feelings. Passion is not success, in my experience. Success is what pays the bills. Don is so passionate that, five years earlier, he had sold his plasma to take me out for dinner on Valentine's day.

"Meet me, just once," Don asks, over the phone, the evening I tell him it is over. He lives two hours away in Madison, Wisconsin. "Just to say goodbye."

The November day we meet is a cold, drizzly one; it cannot be any drearier. A chilly wind whips off of Lake Michigan as I walk from the subway to the appointed coffee shop under a cold, steady drizzle. The weather is appropriate, I think years later, and I wonder if he painted a water color of the spindly, dripping branches and the umbrella-covered passersby we saw as we simply said “goodbye,” skipping the coffee and any discussion.

His patience with me was Olympian, I realize now. Three years into our relationship I was questioning us, yet he was so all accepting; so kind and forthcoming with love. He was, in a way, a victim of my dad’s inability to love—and my fear I was not loveable.

CHAPTER TWELVE

"BOWLING BALLS"

When I am 22, I sell bowling balls for a living.

"It should feel like part of your hand, really," I tell the middle-aged, balding man in Gritzmacher's sporting goods store. He stands before a rack of black orbs seeking the perfect ball for his Wednesday night league. His wife surprised him with the money for his birthday, he tells me, because they joined the league a month ago and she thinks he'll score better with his own ball. "Feel like you're one with the ball," I add.

I don't tell him, or any of the other middle-aged men, that the last time I bowled I was 13, and it was probably one of the worst days of Christmas vacation because I cleared my dad's score, by mistake. An accident, of course, but Dad was already so frustrated because rain had ruined our northern Michigan ski weekend, that I shrank beneath his glare.

"Does this one feel as good as it looks?" I ask the customer, a shirt-and-tie guy who probably worked in management at Nekoosa Paper Mill. I am alone in this small sporting goods store so I can use any glib line I think will work. Though my interest in sales is next to none, the tips I've heard from Dad through the years seem to be part of my psyche. "The next knock on the door will be a sale," he tells me repeatedly when I am 16 and have somehow been cajoled by a friend—ironically her dad is a mentee of my dad's—to carry a burnt-orange and olive-green-flowered vinyl case through neighborhoods, selling Fuller Brush cleaning products.

Selling bowling balls, ski equipment, and ice fishing lures (a sport I know zero about) is a means of paying for a small, one-room apartment in this Wisconsin town where I am given a few newspaper assignments every week. Wisconsin Rapids is two hundred miles away from Don, who is teaching art in the tiny Michigan Upper Peninsula town of Ontonagon, and this is where I can find a newspaper editor willing to hire me part time. It is the closest I can possibly live near Don and have some semblance of the job I want.

After work I perch on bar stools with a handful of reporters and drink twenty-five-cent glasses of draft beer at the Speakeasy Bar. Every weekend I drive the desolate two-lane roads to visit Don.

I do this because I think I have no choice.

I am in love with Don.

But I am at war with Dad and with myself. It is a silent war in which I want to let go and leave behind me all the sterile, cold country clubs and quiet dinners and anxieties of my childhood. I just want to be with Don because he tells me he loves me and I feel like I am the most special person in the world when I am with him.

I cannot be with Don all the time in the small town he lives in because I want a job. But I have to see him because I have to know a man loves me. If Dad can't, doesn't or won't, I will stay with someone who does.

I am still so bound to Dad, thinking I cannot live, or breathe, without his approval. It will be another ten years before I learn to take those really deep guttural breaths, contemplate what works for me, and expel that air with a sense that I do have a choice.

Do I fault Dad, now, for not trying to tell me how foolish I am being, sacrificing a job to accommodate Don, who has chosen this faraway town on nearly the furthest northwestern edge of the Upper Peninsula? In part, yes, because I think truly loving someone means, at times, treading into uncomfortable territory. But Dad is in the middle of making lots of money, taking over a business in Chicago that he will turn around with long hours and focused attention, and retire in ten years in a financial position he wants.

He does what he knows how to do—well. This does not include talking about feelings to his adult children.

On a gray, chilly November afternoon, I walk through the doorway of the Wisconsin Rapids Daily Tribune with newspaper clips from my college internships in hand. An hour later I walk out with the promise of at least three weekly assignments from the affable, middle-aged editor I remember only as Joe; a week later I move into my small, slope-ceilinged, one-room-second-story apartment and look for my second job.

"The skiing is great," my co-worker Sandra, a recently-married, 20-something-year-old, says on a Thursday evening, as she closes out the cash register at the sporting goods store, "We can go for miles and I can show you trails you'll never find on your own." Sandra is athletic, knows the area well, and is very willing to befriend me. She shakes her head when I say, as I do every time she invites me to go skiing, that I am taking off for the weekend. In my rattled old Datsun, I will drive north to visit Don who is living on a miserly budget to pay off college debt.

"Stick around this weekend and come out for dinner with me and my wife," suggests Bill, a tall, personable reporter just five years my senior. I am drinking my third draft beer at the Speakeasy on a Wednesday evening. "By summer, I predict, Joe will have an opening on the staff and hire you. And if you don't want to stay in Rapids forever, there's always the State Journal to make your way down to. This is a great area to live in," Bill adds.

But neither friendly offer can entice me to Make a Life in this friendly Midwestern hamlet.

"I'm doing the best I can!" I scream one morning when I wake up to my breath vaporizing in the frigid air of my apartment, the heat having shut off, once again, because the downstairs tenants argue, fight, split up and neglect to order fuel for the furnace. My car, too, refuses to start on this subzero morning. I have no work that day, so I walk to the newly-opened Rapids Mall. The wind whips my face as my boots make crunching noises on the snow-packed sidewalks.

There is a sidewalk sale within the small, six-store mall. I buy a toddler-sized sweater. It is only $1.99 and my purchase unleashes the cacophony of emotions playing in my mind. It makes no sense, my purchase of this little blue cardigan with its red prancing deer. I try to lose myself in the JC Penney adult clothing—sweaters, pants or anything for me or Don—but I circle back to infants and toddlers. I toss a pint-sized pair of red rubber boots into my cart, and I don't hesitate to make another purchase. I do this because I am 22 years old and dying to have a baby.

"Why," I ask my zoology-major college roommate one day as we are out jogging, "would a nest with babies fall out of a tree like that? Wouldn't the birds be smarter?"

We have come upon a nest on the edge of a busy road with tiny, dead nestlings in it.

"Sometimes the males make bad decisions, but not very often," Jennie says. "Like building too far out on a limb."

The man I love is too far out on a limb for me, I know, when I am 22, because he is passionate about his art. I want to run with that passion, too, but I need the nest I'm used to.

Two days later, a thaw in the weather having allowed my aging Datsun to start again, it is twilight as I approach Ontonagon. Suddenly, I am spinning out of control, my bald tires unable to grip at the icy intersection. I clutch the plastic steering wheel tightly and the blue interior of my little car seems to go blurry as I engage the clutch and try to brake. I am in the midst of a 360—a doughnut, the locals say—as I have hit an icy patch of road. I come to rest seconds later in the middle of the two lanes.

But this doesn't stop me from offering to make the 400-mile round trip every weekend. With my schedule, Don and I can be together three nights, even if on occasion I leave before sunrise for a mid-morning assignment on Monday.

•••———◆

How long can I keep on allowing myself to be held captive? Now, at 65 years old, I want to shake this 22-year-old version of myself, place my hands squarely on her shoulders, and rid her mind of this self-imposed ball and chain.

The toddler sweater and boots are thrust into my closet, and, in fact, it will be fifteen years before I have a baby. The red rubber boots dry up and crack in their JC Penney shopping bag, which I store away in my Life in Boxes. I thrust the little deer-prancing toddler sweater at my sister-in-law one Christmas, gushing out my maudlin tale, and she accepts it for her son, giving me a well-intentioned baleful look that cuts deeply.

I leave for my weekends away by early afternoon on Fridays heading north with a sandwich in hand, driving the two-lane snow-covered highways anticipating my reunion with Don by five p.m., being met by his outstretched arms and an open can of Leinenkugel beer. I stop only once, just after crossing the state line into this crazy part of Michigan that should, by all rights, be attached to Wisconsin. I use the diesel-fumed bathroom at the small gas station and buy a Styrofoam cup of coffee which I will balance precariously between my legs for the rest of the drive. In vending boxes outside the gas station are editions of the *Green Bay Press-Gazette* and *Milwaukee Journal*, and I chuckle at the incongruity of people living in a state where they feel more ties to the state that doesn't govern them. How did this chunk of land, firmly attached to Wisconsin, come to belong to Michigan? Do the residents of this stretch of land know where they belong? Or, like me, do they feel so terribly divided about what they want?

I follow Don's broad back the next afternoon, as we traverse up the snowy, nearly empty trails in the Porcupine Mountains. Lake of the Clouds, a startlingly beautiful pristine body of water nestled between the mountains of this national park, is our destination. "I don't like the job," Don says. "It's not getting any better. But I'm paying my bills. I just have to work until I've saved enough for grad school." Don is burly and an outdoorsman, and an artist who wants only to paint for a living.

"I don't have enough work," I respond. "I'm bored. I don't think I can sell one more goddamn bowling ball!"

We complain to each other and get lost in the company of ourselves, the frigid winds coming at us as we break out of the trees. We create a cocoon every weekend we are together, challenging ourselves to ski longer and harder, then retreating to his tiny apartment, void of furniture beyond a bed and kitchen table, where we eat hotdogs and scrambled eggs and leave only to play pool at the bar down the street.

This little town is, I believe now, a startlingly pristine part of the Upper Midwest that offers solitude. Its population peaked about 1975 at 6,000 people, three years before Don was hired as a teacher in the local school, and I remember meeting fellow teachers of his, some 15 years older than us, who had sought escape from Chicago to live on land with both woods and Lake Superior shoreline. I, however, never learn to truly appreciate its beauty. Rising unemployment will lead to dramatic population decreases after Don's two years there.

There is a weekend I stay in Wisconsin Rapids during the

four months I live there. Betsy visits me from where she is living in Chicago, and we ski, drink beer and for two days I feel as if I have made a life. We sit on my couch, the sloping walls creating an attic-like feel in my small living space. It is Sunday morning, and I am wearing a snowflake-patterned red and white flannel robe I'd ordered from Montgomery Wards for $7.99; an indulgent purchase since I am determined to live as miserly as Don.

"What if," Betsy says to me, "you just went wherever you wanted to go? What if you had taken the job you were offered in Montana?"

"You aren't in love," I say quickly. "You don't understand that I can't go there."

The editor at the *Missoulian* had called me as a result of a query letter I'd sent in June, before Don had found his job. I'd turned down his offer of a job interview within twenty-four hours, quickly rejecting a chance to move to one of the most scenic areas of the country.

I yearn to take Betsy's advice.

"Pick a town, any town," Linda says to six of us gathered in her small apartment, a week later. It is evening, and our small group is feasting on steaming bowls of her homemade chili. Linda, like me, is a recent journalism graduate and has tired of waiting for a full time opening, on a local radio station. We met while covering a story of a farmer and his claim that his multi-toed chickens were a result of birth defects from Wood County's use of DDT on his fields. She'd arrived at the rural farm just as I had talked with the gristly old farmer. After running into each other at a school board meeting the next evening, in which vehement debate ensued about whether to add another November "hunting day" to the school calendar, we'd had a beer.

"Anywhere," Linda says, lifting her glass. "Tomorrow I am 23 and I am giving myself the gift of moving on."

As the beer flows that evening, we all take turns closing our eyes and jabbing our finger on a map of the Midwestern states on Linda's gold carpeted living room floor. She, too, rents a small apartment and her only tie to Wisconsin Rapids is a month-to-month lease.

"Waconia," a grinning, dark-haired man named Stan says as he opens his eyes and looks down at his index finger. It is late enough in the evening that we find the name of the small Minnesota town amusing, and, combined with the beers we have consumed, we decide Linda is to move there by months' end.

Where Linda ended up is a mystery to me, as are the fates of Joe, the middle-aged editor whose keen eyes peered out from thick-rimmed black glasses as he edited my work, and Bill and Sandra.

My sojourn in Wisconsin Rapids lasts four months. I wonder if Mom ever considers asking me to show my dad this scenic North-Woods town? Did they even know I left every weekend? The far-reaching tentacles of my well-meaning mother, enhanced by a very solid network of Chicago area childhood friends and business associates, stretch the two hundred miles from their Barrington home to "my" little town that winter.

Diana tosses her long blond hair and laughs casually, a feminine, careless style I so want to emulate, as she explains why she is moving to Vail.

"To teach skiing for a year or two," she says between bites of roast beef. "I can always sell ski clothes. I want to go out there and ski for a while." Diana, one year older than me, has been a sales representative for a ski clothing manufacturer in Minneapolis, and is home with her parents in Wisconsin Rapids before taking off on her ski bum adventure.

"And we'll be out there visiting, often," adds her Dad. He is relaxed, sipping wine at the head of this antique dining room table. I am in a movie, I think, of a perfect home. "Have to check up on her!"

I am eating a Wednesday evening dinner in this spacious, restored Victorian home because Mom has tracked down a highly-successful businessman connection; the brother-in-law of a high school buddy of Dad's. I watch Diana do another hair flip—her hair extends down her back and stabbingly reminds me of Mom's never-ending refrain to keep my hair short, an edict so strong it follows me most of my life. She flashes her dad a smile and I want to melt into the floor like Dorothy's Wicked Witch.

Why, I want to scream as loudly as I can, does this dad care and mine doesn't?

Does he even love me?

"What a dump!" Diana says cheerfully, as I show her my apartment. It is a week later, and she stops by my apartment, calling up the narrow stairway that she has come to introduce me to high school friends before she leaves. Fashioned out of what was once an attic, the apartment has a tiny bathroom and kitchen. "How do you stand it?"

On an exceptionally cold day in February, I wake up feeling more refreshed than usual, and, on learning my car won't start, I walk a few blocks to go to breakfast. My wool navy pea coat cuts the wind. I eat scrambled eggs at a diner, and walk home to face the tableau of classifieds in my apartment, and with extreme clarity, I know it is time to move on.

I feel no sadness a month later as I leave for a job in LaPorte, Indiana

It will be years before I am able to let go of Don, and many more years before I learn to love Dad without resenting him. Don will love quickly, after we split, but I will need to know I am OK, and lots of time to know I can live just for the sake of living, and that Dad loves me.

I know what love for my children is; a certainty that you will always do what you think is best for them; a protectiveness you feel that makes you know you would never, ever knowingly hurt them. But love between adults is different; intimate love is confusing, wonderful and challenging. I think it will slip into my life easily, but it doesn't.

I do not think of the red boots or toddler sweater too often, as I move from Wisconsin Rapids to LaPorte and back to Wisconsin to the southeastern town of Kenosha, all the while Don and I chasing each other about as a puppy chases its tail. When we walk away from each other, I am not happy about leaving him but relieved because I just know it cannot work. I walk away knowing we are bringing each other pain—that we stretched this gig just a bit too long and didn't leave the party while we were still having a good time.

THE NEWSPAPER GUILD
Affiliated with the AFL-CIO, the CLC
the International Federation of Journalists

Emily Thayer
Name of Member

Kenosha Newspaper Guild # 15
Local Guild

19 84

Intl. Chairperson
Intl. President

Local President

CARD NO. 33 ISSUED January 2, 1981

AMERICAN YOUTH HOSTELS, Inc.
National Office
Delaplane, Virginia 22025
Membership Card

AYH

107186
Card Number

Date of Birth

Senior
Type S

NAME AND ADDRESS Exp. Dec.31,
1981

Emily Thayer
5302 67th Street
Kenosha, Wi. 53142

I agree to abide by the youth hostel regulations of the country in which I am travelling.

CHAPTER THIRTEEN

"LIFE IN BOXES"

Dad is a boss. Betsy, Rob and I know that.

There are many evenings, in Battle Creek, when a younger version of Dad follows him, in a rental car, from the Clark Equipment corporate offices on Battle Creek's northwest side, to our home. Dad does not loosen his tie, as usual, when he brings these protégés of his home, and we eat in the dining room.

"You must love living here," the conversation usually goes, as the young businessman eats my mom's baked chicken and peas. "On a lake and all." The men are confident, like my dad, and strike up a conversation about their wives and children at home, and I remember thinking how clearly defined everyone's roles are.

Dad is the alpha male. I do not see a single woman in my father's business, and as an occasional friend of my mother's ventures beyond homemaking to become a realtor, all I hear from Mom is how awful it would be to have to work, and how she is far too kind to ever hold a job.

My takeaway from all this is that I had better be ready to work in a man's world, but, no worries because if I work for a man, I simply have to do what he asks.

Judge Robert Graham, a graying man who sits on the bench of the LaPorte County Circuit Court in Indiana, is four years older than my dad. I spend a great deal of my time in his courtroom, covering the criminal courts for the LaPorte Herald-Argus in 1979—'80, my first full-time job out of college. I thrive in this position because this judge replaces Dad; he is experienced, confident, captain of the ship. He runs his courtroom in a no-nonsense way. "I think, young man," I recall him saying from high up on the bench, "that you could have paid this fine. You buy record albums, right? You put gas in your motorcycle?"

Judge Graham scares me.

"Read the medical records," my editor instructs me one afternoon. I am in the midst of covering a criminal trial; the defendant is claiming insanity. "They're in the file, in his office. Read them."

The judge's secretary hands me the file; a file I don't want to read because I am not sure it's something I should be seeing, despite my editor's insistence. I sit quietly in a chair next to the secretary's desk in the outer office, scribbling notes as fast as I can.

"Should you be reading that?" Judge Graham enters the office from his chambers and suddenly he is standing next to me. His face is stern, I have the feeling he is admonishing me as a daughter, not a reporter, and my face turns red with embarrassment. "I'm not sure," I stammer. "I was told to read it." "But do you think you should be reading it?" he questions me a second time, and I feel as if I am caught with my hand in the cookie jar. "Would you want someone reading that about you?"

It takes only his stern voice for me to slip my notes away and hand the file back to his secretary, red-faced. I am not clear on the law, but I have no intention of questioning his edict. He is a man.

I slip out of the courthouse building and slink the three blocks back to the newspaper. Some 40 years later I can't remember what I told my boss, or what article I wrote. But I can still feel the happiness—the validation—I feel a few days later when Judge Graham sees me in the hallway and congratulates me on my coverage of the courts. "Maybe you should be getting a raise," he says, smiling benevolently. "I'll talk with your boss."

My boss is a woman; a very intelligent, hard-working woman just two years older than me who pushes me to stop looking upon all men as father-roles who want to help me in my career. I leave LaPorte after a year, with an offer from a larger paper in Kenosha, Wisconsin, where I work for an editor I can pretend is my father. In that way, it is very familiar.

If living in LaPorte, this small, friendly town of 10,000 people, did anything for me, at age 22, it helped me realize I am many years and experiences away from a marriage, mortgage and lunch time discussions about Little League and what shrubs to plant in the backyard.

I took from LaPorte what I could: my first official softball uniform of a jersey with orange and white stripes and orange athletic shorts, and cutting my reporting teeth on jailbreaks, untimely teenage traffic fatalities, and the notorious "negligent homicide" Ford Motor Company criminal trial. I gave little to the northwest Indiana town, I am sure, simply breezing through for a year, drinking coffee from a cup and saucer at the Rexall Drug Store lunch counter, weekday mornings with the county sheriff and deputy prosecuting attorney—middle-aged men with receding hairlines and friendly smiles. I remember only being very grateful for a job and the chance to live on my own.

Mostly I remember LaPorte as the town where I feel the thrill of walking onto a recreational softball field in my first-ever athletic uniform, and the utter calm I feel among the 150-year St. Paul's Episcopal Church where I venture into a church, on my own, for the first time as an adult. It is the beginning of my seeking what will truly become my emotional anchors in life, exercise and spirituality. And I experiment with attending church, with Don, the son of a Methodist minister. We never discuss spirituality. The Episcopal service we attend feels foreign to us, and we leave before the close of it. Yet thirty-five years later I can still recall the overwhelming calmness I felt in that church, with its vibrant stained glass windows. What I am seeking, I don't know and my three years of newspaper reporting in LaPorte, and Kenosha, Wisconsin become a time of many quasi commitments. I wait four years before I enter a church again on my own momentum.

LaPorte, I find, is a wonderful place to play golf, eat hamburgers at New Buffalo, Michigan's Redamak's hamburger restaurant and head to the Indiana Dunes on sunny summer afternoons, and I spend a year living there.

And in the midst of my year, I walk into work early on a Saturday morning and find, within minutes, I am talking with two grieving parents who have lost two of their sons in a horrific traffic accident some fourteen hours earlier. The boys had left their rural home at five p.m. driving on county roads slickened by a March snowstorm. Their car is struck by a freight train at an unmarked crossing and the boys die instantly.

"Even though it hurts so much," Tom Leed, the boys' father and stepfather says that day, "we have a peace and joy. We know where they are." I am interviewing the parents in a small, glass-fronted conference room. I sit across the table from this grieving mom and dad, watching them agonizingly twist paper cups of coffee.

I emphasize the parents' acceptance of the horrific tragedy through their belief in God; the article is headlined "Family says faith will see them through tragedy." I think I help them, just a little bit, and I begin to think there might be something pretty wonderful about believing in God. We can't control all the bad stuff that happens, I realize, but maybe there's a way to get through it.

I would like to know if today, forty years later, their faith is still holding them strong.

> "And anyway, even when you think you're getting away with it, God knows you're lying. God knows everything,"
>
> June says to Beaver in "Beaver's Bad Day. "God is everywhere." Season 1, episode 34.

I know God is everywhere and I know I am cheating myself by refusing to commit to a relationship with God, but

I continue on, not wanting it. I accept the offer in Kenosha, and move, my Life in Boxes once again.

"The pigs fell on the guy and killed him," Andy runs a hand over his close-cropped beard and hands me a one-page, typed sheriff's report. He laughs, an abrupt, hardened kind of choking sound perhaps mastered by years of living as a gay man in the 1970s in a small, blue-collar automobile-factory-dominated town in Wisconsin. A mid-afternoon, late July sun shines on a closed reporter's notebook on his desk. Andy loosens his tie and pushes in his desk chair. "No time for me to find anything else out." He takes a few steps though the nearly empty newsroom of Kenosha News. "What a way for the old guy to go," he says, not hiding his smile.

The 81-year-old farmer died, I learn forty-five minutes later, having suffocated from the barrage of pigs that fell from his truck bed. He had parked on a hill to check on a loose hinge on the tailgate, and when the hinge broke and the tailgate fell down, thirty-five pigs spilled out on top of him.

A young Kenosha County sheriff's deputy is at the dead farmer's home taking photos, when I arrive, and we both shake our heads at the tragedy. The dead farmer's son is driving down from Green Bay, the deputy tells me, and might talk with me.

Like the deputy, I am a rookie and as I drive the bumpy, rural roads back to the newsroom I'm angry that Andy could be both lazy and callous at the tragedy. The two Saturday newsroom shifts—6 a.m. to 2 p.m.; 2 to 10 p.m.—are the least liked and veteran reporters like Andy had pushed for a union vote to base the Monday through Friday shifts on seniority, leaving these Saturday shifts to be covered every week by the two newest reporters. His campaign had failed, and he, as did a few other long-time reporters, essentially did little work on their Saturday shifts, in revenge.

"Friday night," Tony says to me Thursday morning at work. "At my house, seven p.m., bring your own beer." Tony lifts the bright blue plastic cup holder and drains his last few sips of coffee from the white plastic insert. "Gotta go back up," he says and smiles, and grabs his brown cardigan from the back of the chair in the break room. I'm on my ten-minute coffee break and the 63-year-old Tony has to get back up to the newsroom to pick up last-minute obits that might come in before the eleven a.m. deadline.

There is always a steady stream of Red, White and Blue beer flowing at Tony's Friday night poker games and I enjoy the evening—bringing my Michelob Light—because it's a chance for me to take risks in the warm cocoon of Tony's two-story clapboard bungalow. Tony is a kind, grandfatherly-type who is eager to make friends with the reporters. A pressman for years, he is transferred to the newsroom when the owner of the Kenosha News modernizes from using hot lead and setting type, to offset printing in the late 1970s. Tony charms us with his stories of growing up on the south side of Chicago. He also starts a daily quarter toss with anyone present in the newsroom, when the city editor signs off on the edition to the press operators every day about noon.

But my delight with Friday night poker games and daily quarter tosses are not enough to keep me from feeling trapped in this town. Mostly I feel so governed by the heavy hand of the union I must pay dues to that I need to leave. I am too young to cover an evening city council meeting and be forced to wait until morning to write the story, avoiding additional overtime. I can't watch the games reporters play anymore as they extend their allowed ten-minute morning coffee break to twenty and thirty minutes.

I am reading the *Chicago Tribune* on a Sunday afternoon in my Kenosha apartment, and in the Budget Traveler column I see a nugget about inexpensive fare on the Queen Elizabeth II cruise ship, for travelers under age 25, between New York City and Southampton, England.

I am out of Kenosha. I run off to Europe when opportunity arises.

If there is one thing my college friend Jennie does, it is to simplify.

"I'm wearing socks with my sandals so I had one less pair of socks to pack,' Jennie announces as we leave our closet-sized state room on the Queen Elizabeth II to go to our first dinner.

This five-day trip across the Atlantic Ocean lands us with bicycles and backpacks in South Hampton, England. I have a three-month Eurail pass, and plan to traverse several countries after biking with Jennie for two weeks in England. I plan to store, or sell my bike after she leaves England to return home. I have only a one-way ticket on the QEII and plan to fly home.

It is all quite spontaneous, this European trip. It takes only a few days to convince myself to tell my editor my plans to leave my job in two weeks, buy my ticket and Eurail pass and talk myself out of an apartment lease. My friend Jennie's decision to come with me for two weeks was also reached quickly.

Five days on a luxury liner, with three meals served on china by uniformed waiters, and dining companions all under 25 years old seeking a lark in Europe, is fun. By day three I am spending little time with Jennie and most of my time with a young man I remember only as Gabe, an Englishman returning to university after a summer of beaches in the United States. Arrival at our destination is on a chilly October Saturday evening, and as Jennie and I wheel our bikes off the ship, backpacks on, I get a sinking feeling that I am seeking fun on this trip, and perhaps not with her.

We chat that evening, and both of us being adventurous, impulsive and selfish, we part company the next morning, with tentative plans to meet three days later in London. We decide not to meet up and travel together, and the trip becomes, for me, a quest to forget Don, to whom I am still writing letters. I traverse England with one man, southern France with another, and meet a third man to go to Greece with me. Names do not matter. I am only seeking their company.

I am seeking a deeper connection with myself. I learned

that while I can travel alone or spend a few days traveling with men I meet, I made a grave error in not trying to continue traveling with my friend Jennie. I learned that I cannot escape myself in Europe.

When I return, after three months of aimless wandering in Europe, ending with my lack of patience in Athens, Greece with an international phone system that made it challenging to reach Don, I have only my parents to turn to. They generously welcome me into their home for the holidays, but it is clear to all of us that I need a job and an independent life. I get a job and apartment in Chicago, and, finally, as I turn 26, I take the step needed to move on with my life.

When I break up with Don, it is a goodbye where we both realize we can never be friends, and I leave the coffee shop with such extreme feelings of joy and sadness that I know it was not a love that could be sustained.

I will find that I can't love a man—really love him—until I tame my demons of anxiety, and accept Dad.

"I thought, like, maybe, you were interested too," my date, two years later, says as he gets up from my nubby brown couch and heads to the door of my studio apartment. "I mean, you said you were and I thought..." his voice trails off, and I realize I have once again misjudged my desires. Scott is nice, older than me, pleasant and interesting. We have dated several weeks, and just as we begin to get close, I pull away.

What is it I want? He is a man Dad would approve of, and while I find myself seeking such men, I also find myself equally unattracted to that very stability. I am so very scared of a lack of emotion from any man who is financially secure.

I won't go through my adult life not knowing if the man I chose to marry really loves me. And right now, I cannot believe that a man who is stable and secure knows how to express anything other than what he wants.

This, I've got to figure out.

CHAPTER FOURTEEN
"NEW SUIT"

"Tickets along the third-base line," tall, sandy-haired Peter, a security officer at MacNeal Hospital, says. I have worked late and he is driving me to the off-site parking lot. "They're for this Saturday. Wanna go?"

Peter, I find out from co-workers, is taking college classes during the day, working security third shift, living at home and recently gave his mother enough money to remodel her kitchen.

"My dad bought these tickets when I was born," Peter says from our seats along the third base line at Comiskey Park, three days later. "We went to almost every home White Sox game until last summer."

"He had a heart attack on the Fourth of July," Peter adds.

From our seats I can hear the third baseman taunting the batter; the sun is high in the sky and all around us avid fans have their radios tuned to the Chicago station carrying the game. The sweat from the runner to home base practically flies off his brow onto us, we are so close to the players.

Peter is generous, and fun, but I simply add Peter to my list of nice guys who ask me out. I am 28, two years free of my extended college relationship with Don, and still scared of my dad.

I say yes just to see how many men find me attractive enough to want to go out with me. I am treating dating the same way many people shop for new cars. Take a look at what's available, spend a little time with each just to see how the ride feels, and move on.

I am sampling all the single men when all I really want is to ask Dad if he loves me.

Berwyn, Illinois is a small town, and when I interview for a job in public relations at MacNeal Hospital in 1984, I have walked into an opportunity to learn the business. The board of directors of this once sleepy hospital has decided to compete for business with neighboring suburban hospitals, and money is poured into public relations and marketing. I am hired by a 30-something-year-old businessman eager to make his mark, and I learn, essentially, how to spend money, producing glossy brochures, magazines and advertisements. I work well with the mostly all-male medical staff, and I thrive, for a while, in this environment of jumping through hoops, for men, for a good salary.

I meet Scott, 10 years older, a successful architect. He owns a house and has never been married. We meet though the Chicago Outings Club.

There is a Saturday, in December, when I am 29 years old and I think Scott is the man I want to marry.

I wander through Marshall Fields on that Saturday afternoon, excited because that evening I am going to a Christmas party at the Hyatt Hotel on Michigan Avenue.

It is my company party, and I am included with upper management because my hospital publications have won regional awards. When I see the bright blue angora scarf, I know it is what I need and that evening as Scott and I walk the four blocks to the party, from my apartment, I think I have made it. I am walking into a party of people who are successful, with a man who is successful, and I am wearing the clothes my dad has been pushing me to buy for years. My soft wool coat drapes my body; my high heels look good and I have on a red and white dress. The blue scarf makes me feel different. I have reached a point in my career, in 1985, where I wear suits to work. One day I leave work early for an appointment in downtown Chicago, and as I walk down State Street, I catch my reflection in a store window. My soft brown leather pumps match the Coach purse hanging from my shoulder; my long wool coat makes me feel tall and thin, and underneath I wear a brown wool suit with a cream-colored silk blouse. I have become the clone of my dad; on this day I feel so satisfied.

At the party, we dance, Scott and I, and we chat with others, and we walk home through the icy wind to my apartment, my blue scarf brightening the night.

"No.... I'm not really serious about you," I say to Scott minutes later at my door. "We're just kinda having fun, ya know, just goofing around."

I can't do it—be what Dad wants—because he pisses me off. I am wearing the brown suit and dating the man with a job and a house because if I do this Dad will love me. Adding a dash of color—a bright blue scarf next to my brown coat—isn't enough, though I'd tried to convince myself when

I bought it that just being a little different would make me feel unique enough to stay on this corporate path. But I am not me; I feel I am what Dad wants me to be.

Scott, frustrated and confused, shoots me a hard, puzzled look, starts to reach towards me again, and suddenly, abruptly turns away and strides towards the elevator. "Well you sure fooled me," he says in a hard-edged, angry voice. "You played games."

How big of a tally in this "men-who-ask-me-out-and-then-I-reject-them" game do I need?

Years later, my husband Tim and I are dressing for his employee Christmas party. It is the mid-1990s, and we are to spend the evening with the people he works with, in a corporate setting, and I know I can't pull off the spiky-heeled boots from Payless. They are the boots I will wear with my girlfriends; the boots I may wear once Tim is retired and we don't have to play the game. It's OK for me to play the game now, because we play it at a minor league level, not the pros, like my parents did. We don't join a country club; we don't buy a fancy house. I know Tim loves me, I know he struggles with how much he has to work, and laments missing some evenings at home with his family. I know this because I finally learned it's OK to ask what he is thinking and feeling.

It never occurs to me, all through my twenties, to ask Dad if he loves me. There is something so very instinctive, and fundamental, about our need to feel loved. Yet I still don't know, in my twenties, if Dad will love me if I don't meet his standards.

Why didn't I ask?

I cannot date enough men after my break-up with my college boyfriend Don. I must prove to myself that I am attractive, loveable and sought after. I am lucky I did nothing more than anger a few people, and learn how to nurture myself through several failed relationships.

How hard Dad tries to show that he loves me, without uttering those three words, and how unaware I am, at the time, that he is trying.

"Try another one," Dad says firmly and quietly, ignoring my frustration over the ill-fitting cut of the women's suit I am trying on. "One will fit." It is a chilly January Saturday; Dad and I are in a suburban Brooks Brothers store where he is buying me a suit to celebrate a job offer from a Chicago public relations firm. My five-foot-four-inch frame is somewhat hard to fit; I rarely shop in expensive stores, nor have I learned to seek out petite sizes, and I easily give up on the rare occasion I try to buy myself well-fitting clothes.

I am 28 years old. Dad has never bought me clothes before. Ever.

Never have I known Dad to indulge in, or even tolerate, my moments of frustration. He simply ignores them.

When I was six, Dad and the rest of my family left me at a state park, alone. "Jump down. Now." Dad stood with car keys in hand. "We're leaving."

A tepid April sun shines down on the stone staircase at

Devil's Rock State Park. We were on a weekend trip and have just spent an afternoon running and playing on the trails.

"I can't," I said. "It's too high. Robbie told me to climb up here, but it's too high to jump down."

Mom had already told me to jump off the rocks we climbed on, near the parking lot. Twice.

"Just cuz Robbie did it doesn't mean I can," I whined. I started crying. "I need help."

My sobs were loud, as I stood at the base of the rocks five minutes later, alone. Mom, Dad, Betsy and Robbie had driven off in the brown Buick.

Will someone else want me? I thought.

They sent Robbie from the car to come back to get me 10 minutes later, after they circled back for me.

> "How did you feel, when your father didn't come after you?" Beaver asks Ward. "Well, I guess I felt pretty bad," Ward says. "I made a mistake, Beaver. I guess that I was so anxious to be right that I... I kind of forgot what it felt like to be a little boy."
>
> "Beaver Runs Away," season 1, episode 37.

Here in the store, I want to throw the suit on the dressing room floor, and walk out of the store with an "I don't deserve it anyway" attitude. I want Dad to give up on me.

"Try another one," Dad insists. My father is not a quitter.

He is steady, prone to neither anger nor delight, and highly dependable. He finishes a task he starts, and only rarely throws in the towel and cuts his losses.

Several suits later, I find an expensive, close-fitting hound's tooth skirt and suit coat that do, in fact, hug my short, stocky frame and look as if they were tailored for me. I recall the satisfaction on Dad's face when we find the suit, but at the time, I am simply relieved that we meet his goal.

Did I know that Dad's quiet, steadfast, deep love for me is expressed through his actions, and not his words?

My boyfriend-shopping lifestyle while working at MacNeal is not made easier by the fact I can't work for a woman. My second female boss I find threatening—most likely because she is pushing me to ask questions of mostly male sources that scare me—is at the *Pioneer Press* where I am a reporter for two years. When I leave there for a position at the hospital, I happily go to work for two men.

There, with a boyfriend search after hours, I am successfully feeding my anxiety with daily doses of striving to please the Male.

This, I know how to do. Listen to what the man in charge wants, respond and out-perform your co-workers, and receive pats on the back. I thrive, for a year, with the publications I produce winning awards and my boss smiling every time he sees me in the elevator. It is so easy; I simply interview male physicians and write about their successes.

It is easy, but only for a while. There appears, on my mother's side of the family, to be a pattern of the women making sacrifices and essentially handing over any influence they had in decision-making to their husbands.

Perhaps I can trace this to my great-great-grandmother, a woman who found herself unwillingly riding a mule across the straits of Isthmus in 1850, a machete clutched in her right hand for breaking the bush and destroying unfriendly reptiles. In her twenties, recently married and without children, she is accompanying her husband from Boston to San Francisco where he intends to sell leather gloves and supplies to the men flooding into California in search of gold.

They returned to Boston several years later, with three children and a substantial bank account. Apparently, men in search of gold wore through many pairs of leather gloves, and many other items, in their quest, and Martha and her husband, Moses Ellis, bought a large house in Framingham, outside of Boston, and she vows she would never travel again. Moses travels in Europe, able to retire on his wise investments, and brought home paintings, china and dolls for his daughters, which my grandmother inherits.

There is a void of knowledge about Grace, my great-grandmother whose parents were Martha and Moses, though we know she left Boston with her husband to settle in Evanston. Her daughter, my grandmother, born in Evanston in 1896, would leave every significant decision in her life in the hands of her father, a Chicago area businessman, or her husband, an investment banker.

Gram, who provides her 12 grandchildren with worship-like devotion until her demise to Alzheimer's at 80 years old, would tell my mother that she simply does not know how to raise a daughter. Her three sons, she told Mom, are easy to raise. "I don't know how to raise you," Mom was told as a young girl. "I just don't know how to raise a girl."

Mom was a dark-haired, brown-eyed energetic four-year-old when her brother George was born. He is named for his father. With his blond curls and blue eyes, attention quickly turned to him. Eighteen months later another son was born; a year later, red-haired Tommy is born. Nancy, seven, turns to her quick-witted father for attention, and received it, and was raised, in the 1930s, by a father who taught her to stake out her territory and hold fast.

In a vacation photo of the four siblings, my mother sits on the edge of a dock in white shorts and T-shirt, a confident grin on her 14-year-old face. Her three brothers perch next to her. George, 10, squints into the sun with a lopsided smile, wearing an argyle sweater and blue jeans. Dick doesn't even smile, sitting upright on the edge of the dock and squinting. But youngest brother Tommy, at seven years old, smiles broadly with a gap-toothed grin. Nancy and Tommy sandwich the two middle boys, as if retaining them on the dock long enough for their dad to shoot the photo.

My mother will spend many of her teenage years teasing her brother George, who simply sailed through his childhood, according to Mom, doing as he was asked. A jealousy, I suppose, incited Mom to taunt him and slam her bedroom door in his face. Mom was a competitive child; the one who always wanted to be first in line and to tell the funniest joke. She doted on her youngest brother Tommy.

By the time Mom left for Connecticut College in 1943, she is regarded by her father as a bright, intelligent young woman and leaves her younger brothers with a sense of peace. She relies on her mother for little, and knows she has an iron-clad supporter in her father. When my grandfather died, when Mom is 59 years old, she told me she had lost her biggest fan.

My mother learned, as a child, to take the brass ring, and found the support she needed to do that in her father, with her mother caught up in raising three sons and running a large household. It was a time of dinner parties and a polished household, despite a nationwide depression; the Great Depression touches my mother's household very little.

"The bums would put a mark on our back fence, on the alley," Mom recalls. "They'd come to our door, asking for money, and we'd give them a ticket to dinner at the Salvation Army. They had different symbols they'd leave on the fence, for what was given out." But day-to-day life remained normal for Mom and her three brothers, not really changing until the outbreak of World War II.

I look at the photo of Mom on her wedding day, in 1949, walking down the steps of their Evanston home in her wedding dress, holding the arm of my tuxedo-wearing grandfather in top hat and tails. She holds a short white coat about her shoulders with one arm, to ward off the late afternoon chill of the April day. It is a Friday evening wedding; a decision by my dad so that they can have a full week's vacation for a honeymoon. My grandfather gazes at Mom with adoration; she is his pride and joy because he has raised her to be stronger than his wife. He also, Mom says, is most likely relieved that his daughter, soon to be 25 years old, has found a husband.

Mom learns to make her needs known, early in her marriage, and she has a confidence I can only marvel at. What takes me many years to express to my husband, she is able to voice early on. She is born, I believe, with a personality free of the anxiety that plagues me, and plagued my grandmother, who found, at times while raising four children, she simply could not cope and would have her children stay with relatives for short bouts while she recovered in bed. My mother is blessed with a personality that allows her to stand her ground and believe in herself.

"We call it 'pink-collar poverty,'" Kate, a specialist in the personnel department at MacNeal Hospital tells me one morning, as she explains new health insurance options to me, for a brochure. "We really want our benefits to stand out because we're finding there's a whole population of women who, divorced and with no job experience, need to find an entry level job. And these are women in their forties."

"For real?" I think as I scribble down comments and gather the handouts Kate has for me. Kate is my age, single, paying off graduate school loans and about to buy a condominium in Chicago. I tell her I have enough information and leave her cubicle.

Kate will be CEO of her own human resources consulting firm within 15 years, and a good friend I come to rely on for advice. "Don't count on your boss being your only advocate," she warns me over drinks one evening, after I've been at the hospital for a year. "You need to find more support."

I am so woefully ignorant of alliances and back-stabbing in the business world that it is a blast out of nowhere when my new boss, in my second year—a middle-aged woman trying to regain professional ground lost through years of stay-at-home-momming—shoves me into a corner.

"Another mistake," she says to me from behind her massive desk, "and I'll have to let you go." A lead ball falls in my stomach; I look up at this 50-something-year-old woman to gauge the seriousness of her intent. She is the new marketing director; my boss having successfully moved himself to a vice-president level. Her intense look into my eyes tells me I am doomed.

I have misidentified a physician in a newsletter caption, a mistake made more grievous by the fact the name is of ethnic descent, and sensitivities of this nature abound within the hospital community. It is a mistake, plain and simple, and one for which my boss clearly receives a verbal beating.

"I had three people proofread..." She cuts off my defense and waves me out of her office. "You're the editor. You have no excuse."

I am, in retrospect, a victim; the lowest member of the food chain in our PR department and hung out to dry. I am naive and know only how to be honest and have not yet learned to find an ally in someone above my boss.

The next morning, I resign. I resign, so that she can't fire me. *I'll* be in charge, thank you very much, even if it means walking away from a good-paying job allowing me to live in Chicago.

Why couldn't I face this woman and ask for support? Why did I walk. Why did I give in to her? Why didn't I call my father at his office, an hour away, and ask the advice of his personnel manager?

"You really messed up?" Wally asks Beaver. "Yeah, I was real crummy," Beaver says.

"It's awfully hard to come to your father and tell him you're no good," Wally explains to Ward.

"The Younger Brother," season 5, episode 28.

CHAPTER FIFTEEN
HOMESTEADING

"It's that rush you get," I tell people, "when you've hiked in the mountains and you reach the top of a peak and the cold winds and the view hit you, all at once."

That is what I say when people ask me why I moved to Vermont.

I don't tell them that I move to Vermont because I am 30 years old and I haven't broken away from my parents, or the Midwest. Or that I feel maybe Dad will love me more if I prove to him I can make it on my own. I can stake my own territory; lay claim to my own homestead.

I can show him I don't need him. My decision to move from Chicago to Williston, Vermont is made fairly quickly, and easily. My best friend Amy has recently bought a two-bedroom home, a converted one-room schoolhouse where afternoon sun shines through the former classroom windows, and a wood-burning stove fueled by a massive woodpile keeps us warm. I love the mountains, and latch onto the feeling of coming home, with my grandmother's stories of summers spent in nearby Charlotte in my memory.

As I leave Chicago to move in with Amy, my friend Kate warns me there will be fewer jobs in Vermont and that I have connections in the Chicago area, and offers to coach me in finding a job locally. She is a good friend, and years later I will think how patient she was with my impulsiveness. I just know I need to try to get away from the lingering shadow of searching for Dad's approval.

I am lucky that I can rely on my friend Amy. She charges me little rent, and I am able to eke out a living for a couple of years as a freelance writer.

Initially, I assume a job at a construction company, in communications, because it is practical. I even turn down a job in public relations at the hospital in Burlington because it is part-time. It's a very poor decision, not at all based on emotion, and I do not do well in the corporate environment.

In my three months' tenure, I managed to loose the company's expensive camera, leaving it in a bar I go to after attending an evening photography class. I also alienated a handful of the engineers one morning, the day after election, in November, when I try to chat about the fact Vermont voters failed to pass the ERA, in the confined space of the company's private plane, en route to Portland, Maine.

It is not the environment for me, and we part mutually after the first of the year.

Fortunately, the good-hearted PR director at the hospital feeds me plenty of freelance work, and my freelance business takes off.

I am a good writer, there is no question. I am not a particularly adept business person, and I never move beyond writing copy, billing my clients, and paying my bills. My biggest business move is paying a small monthly fee for a downtown Burlington business address, phone number and person to answer my calls to give the impression I have a downtown office.

•••———◆

"Let's put it on paper," Dad and I are finishing a glass of wine, enjoying the sunset over Lake Champlain on a winter evening. I have been living in Vermont for a year. Recently retired, Dad has come to visit me for a long weekend. We have come for a drink in Burlington's highest office building, the top floor of a recently-constructed building meant to complement Burlington's pedestrian mall. It's been a good evening; I picked him up at the airport, showed him my quasi "office" where I pick up phone messages, and introduced him to others using the space. We have been talking about his and my mom's recent move to Florida, and he is flush with contentment over this new phase of his life.

I am telling him I need to take a next step, renting a real office where I can work, moving my computer out of my bedroom.

Did I want Dad to be kind to me that evening, perhaps even offering to cover some of my business rent? He is frank—honest—and the figures that dance before my eyes fifteen minutes later show me I cannot afford an office, unless I am better able to flush out higher-paying jobs than I have. Mostly, my writing jobs are small potatoes. Am I willing to be more aggressive, work harder and only take the good-paying jobs? Dad asks. Am I ready to compete against other writers, and stop picking up the dregs they leave me once they have moved on?

I only cry a little, at the restaurant, and we leave to go home. Dad is honest with me, showing me the numbers, and I leave feeling I don't have the confidence to take my work to the next level. Now, I realize I did.

The job I land in Burlington, a few months later pays well and is in my field. I interview with the eager, young new CEO of the former Fanny Allen Hospital, then an independent Catholic hospital trying unsuccessfully to compete against the medical center associated with the University of Vermont. I take the offer, convinced I will be working for a man and slipping into the role I once thrived in, back in Berwyn.

On a drive to Montreal, Quebec on an early Friday morning, two years later, I feel a familiar panic and must pull over on the seventy-mile drive north to calm myself. In my mind, I am facing my boss again, back in her office in Berwyn, being given an ultimatum.

I am on my way to a business retreat in a Montreal hotel for the hospital's board of directors and top administrators. The Canadian city is being chosen because the hospital's owners, a religious order of nuns, is headquartered in Montreal. I am driving alone because I have been asked, at the last minute, to attend the meeting.

"Come on up to the meeting," says Bill as he calls me into his office the day before. "Record the meeting and just listen to what we're talking about. I want you to know what's going on. It may be too late to get in on a car pool, but come on up for the day."

I am not respected by the administrators. Again, most are female and I have failed miserably at working with them.

Once Bill has hired me, he has me work for an experienced, older woman who has her own agenda. Apparently, I learned nothing from my experience in Berwyn, from which I had fled, and I don't seek out a mentor or, married at this point, ask my husband for advice. I simply flounder. Bill remains loyal to me yet he, too, is dealing with his own struggles and can offer me little help.

I drive alone to Montreal. I find the hotel, park and arrive in the conference room a few minutes late. Bill nods in a friendly way, and I set up my tape recorder in a corner. I do not expect anyone to make small talk with me during the breaks, yet an inner confidence from somewhere within has me chatting with the board members. I am not willing to relegate myself to simply support staff, a naive move on my part that infuriates my immediate boss. I look back at myself proudly, because I did what I was able to do to take care of myself. I didn't know how to work with women, and for that I am sorry and embarrassed. But I did know how to talk with businessmen; how to listen to them and show interest—and I did just that.

That evening, Bill asks me to stay for dinner with the group. I stay, and by evening's end at 11 p.m., I do not want to drive home. "Can I share a room?" I ask several of the women attending the meeting. The next morning, over coffee in the lobby, I thank the person who allowed me to have her room; she opted to share with another colleague. We are alone, and she smiles at me, hesitates as if she wants to say something, and then simply says, "You're welcome," and excuses herself.

I will be asked to leave the job, a month later. I am

pregnant; it is not a time I want to quit a job and look for another one. Financially, I get a good offer in the separation and Bill takes me into his office before I leave and advises me to look forward.

I am left, once again, wondering how I screwed up. What am I doing wrong?

CHAPTER SIXTEEN
"ANGER AT LAST"

"Dad, I gotta buy gifts this Christmas, too." My breath comes out in little puffs in the frigid air. We're at Old Orchard Center, a fairly new cluster of upper-end stores linked by a web of attractively-landscaped sidewalks, in Skokie. It is 1965 and I am nine.

"Christmas sure is better when you don't have to buy stuff, isn't it?" I add, looking up at my dad. We are shopping together on a December morning because I am the child assigned by Mom to help him with his annual shopping event. The walks have been cleared of snow and the trees are eerily bereft of leaves. The bubbling fountain outside Marshall Field's has been turned off and the concrete pond is empty. Dad is laden with Mom's gifts in three small shopping bags, and I am carrying his new wing tips from Chandlers. Shoppers bustle by. In this moment, under the gray December sky, I feel like I can tell my dad anything.

"Not just stuff for Betsy and Robbie, this year, but for you and Mom, too. Mom told me. I asked her cuz Mr. Richardson said at Sunday School we're supposed to be ready way before Christmas. So we can help our moms."

I am so excited in this epiphany and oh, so anticipating

Dad's reaction when he realizes we are brethren; that I feel his pain in slogging through stores on a December Saturday, and that I, too, have to spend my hard-earned money on gifts.

"Don't you know the *meaning* of Christmas?"

Dad's response is in an ice-brick tone of a voice; it freezes my heart and lodges deep down in my gut. He stops walking, and his eyes pierce right through my sky-blue parka; I clutch my shopping bag tighter and scrunch my other hand around the green snowflake-patterned trim next to my zipper. Dad doesn't want an answer. I curl into an imaginary ball in my head, right there on the sidewalk next to Carson Pirie Scott, and think if I scrunch my right hand hard around my jacket, the abyss inside me—the big, black dark hole inside me because Dad doesn't love me—will disappear.

Dad and I drive home.

This Saturday morning burst of anger toward me in 1965 is one of the two times I can recall when Dad gets angry with me as a child. It hurts—very badly—because on both occasions when this happens, I am sharing with him some newly-mined nugget of knowledge in my young brain that I think will make him love me. I am showing him we are kindred spirits.

> "Ward, the only guide the little fellow has is the love and approval of his parents. Now if he thinks he's lost that, then it's worse than a beating," June to Ward. "I guess that's one of the troubles of being a parent," Ward replies. "You love your kids so much you scare the pants off of them." "
>
> The Haircut," season 1, episode 4.

"I suppose I have to," Dad says to Mom the night before his Saturday-before-Christmas shopping trip, when she reminds him Christmas is three days away. Dad will not veer from her list, nor will he suggest we look in the toy department at Marshall Fields or sip hot chocolate at the Walgreens soda counter. But he is happy that morning because he is doing what is expected of him. I am the buffer between the department store sales clerks and him, a reluctant shopper. I am the child assigned by Mom to help him buy precisely what she has written on a list for her for Christmas.

I like the shopping trip, even though I am nervous that I will say something he doesn't want to hear, like Robbie drew a mustache in Magic Marker on my Little Lulu doll, or I'm way behind in my math workbook. I like to sit in the front seat of the car with Dad and know that I am alone with him. Even if he doesn't talk, I know he is my Dad and I belong to him and for these brief hours there are no expectations for me, except for one. I can't ask a question that Dad would consider "dumb." My questions to Dad must be well thought-out; I must think real hard about whether I already know the answer.

I guess I told Dad something dumb today. I guess I can't do that, either.

> "Gee, it's hard to believe that anybody's father really knows what's going on in a kid's mind," Beaver says to Ward. "Well, it doesn't take much doing," Ward says.
>
> "More Blessed to Give," season 6, episode 18.

Despite all my Sunday mornings in class with someone's dad droning on about this Jesus guy, or sitting next to Baba in church playing tic-tac-toe, I am obviously lacking in any real knowledge of Christmas. I learn, from my attendance at Covenant Methodist Church until I am 10, the following:

We are always late if Mom leaves first, alone, to go to choir practice.

Betsy will not take me all the way to my classroom after the first week, even if the stairs are very dark and quiet, and I beg her.

*In second grade, if I wear the sailor dress with a whistle around the neck (**not** a church dress but I can sneak it by Dad), I am happy trying to take the little ball out of the whistle hole for forty-five minutes, until the teacher yells at me to stop and tells me never to wear that dress again.*

If I am not late (when Mom skips choir), I can sometimes sit next to Clark Weber's daughter who is the only girl I try to become friends with, ever, because all my friends in Winnetka go to church in Winnetka. Her dad is a DJ on a radio station and he gives away free 45s on Halloween. She is really cool.

When we pass by the big sign on Green Bay Road for a moving company, painted on the brick building with a boy in a striped T-shirt pulling a little boy in a wagon, holding toys, I know we are almost there and my heart starts pounding.

We never go into the new room after church where Betsy says you get to eat coffee cake and everyone is there and you talk to people.

Dad always wants to go straight home.

I hafta bring in a dime from my allowance every week for the collection.

In summer when we drive to church with the top down, Dad has to put it up on the way there so Mom won't ruin her hair-do (there is no choir in summer).

We just always, always go—except never on vacation—and I don't know why.

I feel good afterwards.

At all my Sunday School classes held in a warren of small, dark rooms with low tables and chairs, Mr. Richardson —or other dads—tell us stories about men with funny names like Moses and Jonah, and we color with broken crayons. Only when Clark Weber's daughter convinces her dad to teach a class do we pay attention. Clark Weber will be the first Chicago DJ to play the Beatles on Chicago area radio and is the coolest dad I know.

Obviously, I somehow fail to pay attention in Sunday School when someone's dad tells us Christmas is a Christian holiday; that it is the birthdate of Jesus and that Christmas gift giving is symbolic of love and of the gifts given by the three Wise Men to Jesus. That message goes right over my head. Sitting next to Clark Weber's daughter or even just knowing she lives in the same house as Clark Weber consumes many of my Sunday school thoughts.

Christmas, up until this year, has been all about the Sears

and Roebuck catalogue toy section and making a list for Mom and eating real mashed potatoes and rolls with butter and sugar cookies, with my cousins. That has been quite enough to satiate me.

When my husband Tim and I experience those moments of feeling a kindred tie—when we know the stars have aligned and we understand each other's feelings and can respond with empathy, even if in our eyes, only—I feel so very alright; there is no better feeling. That was the feeling I was striving for, on that Saturday in December, 1965, when I shared my new "burden" of gift giving with Dad.

In my innocent question to Dad on that Saturday morning, I reveal the duplicity of his actions; brought into the open his true thoughts. Does he analyze that moment? Does he realize what I have learned by virtue of paying more attention to the cues at home than the forced-upon-me-sitting-in-a-church-dress Sunday School lessons?

Does he not admit this mistake because he doesn't realize it or is it because he is too scared to do so?

> "Well, anyway son, I'm sorry,"
>
> Ward to Wally, "Wally's Election," season 3, episode 19.

> "Beaver, I've made a lot of mistakes in my life but I've never made one that it didn't at least help to say 'I'm sorry.'
>
> Ward to Beaver, "Wally's Birthday," season 2, episode 1.

Christmas is, in our family, while obviously lacking in my young years of any talk of Jesus or giving gifts out of love, a tremendous suspension of reality. Preparation for this momentous event totally falls on Mom, and she shoulders the responsibility well. For at least a solid week when I am young, our kitchen table is dedicated to cutting out sugar cookies in the shapes of stars and trees and Santas, and decorating them, after school. We give them to teachers, neighbors, relatives, babysitters, the milkman, the paperboy and the mailman.

In the 1960s, Christmas at our house is a total Mom affair, and she pulls it off with aplomb, complete with decorating the tree after we are in bed on Christmas Eve, leading us to believe Santa does the job. I don't know if Dad helps her; I know his excitement of this day—Christmas Day in which he suspends reality—mounts the day before.

We arrive at Gram and Gramp's house by four, and my Uncle Tom is already happily mixing drinks in the butler's pantry. Trays of triangle sandwiches and curlicue-cut carrots lie on silver trays ready for my great-aunt to pass. Though itchy in my smocked holiday dress, the warmth of Gram hugging us as we run through the chilly vestibule and into their cigarette-scented house outweighs that discomfort. It is always a challenge to know where to go first in this oasis of a home—to say hi to Rosa cooking in the kitchen, to the sun porch to play with small, funny-looking dolls Gram's grandfather brought her from Europe, or to the bookcase full of parchment rolls to play 1920s foxtrots on the massive player piano. And on the third floor of this house is my Great-Aunt Bey's slope-walled room with easels, oil and tempera paints and modeling clay we may play with at will. It is a house my grandmother lives in her entire life.

Visits here are brief, at holidays. A gathering of twelve or more with aunts and uncles and cousins is overwhelming to him; Mom honors his need to take her family in short bursts.

Dad will mix, a bit, in the flower-wallpapered living room with its chintz-covered couches and grand piano. My aunts and uncles are bubbly and full of talk, relaxed by Irish coffees and gin and tonics, and I love the feeling of being with my tribe. Gram is a charmer, warming everyone with her engaging smile, and Dad genuinely loves her embracing comments. They are my people, my cousins Carol, Nancy and Tommy and the others. On Christmas eve, we each open a gift from Gram and Gramp and Great-Aunt Bey, placing our small stash protectively, lovingly in a safe place under an end table or arm chair. The glint of silver from the massive dining room table in a room anchored by leaded bay windows at one end and credenza with silver pheasants at the other, catches my eye. It is set for the holiday dinner on the next day. We will not come; the agreement is Christmas day with the small, quiet group of Thayer relatives. But at this dining room table, I eat many Thanksgiving dinners.

"Up in the sky," Dad says. He is driving us home, and I am bursting with excitement for the day that is to follow. I strain my neck and push into my sister to try to see out the passenger window. "Listen," Dad says. "On the radio, he says there's lights up there, and something like a sleigh." Dad slows as we drive north on Sheridan Road, telling us to keep peering up and we will see Santa. This is pure bliss, and I will play along with this fable for as long as I can. When we pull into our driveway minutes later, Dad skips the floor pads-seatbelts routine.

"Not yet," Dad says on Christmas morning as we try to peer into the living room from the bend in our stairs. "I think he might still be here." When we are released, we tug down our bulging stockings from the fireplace mantel; Dad's involvement slips into that of a bystander as the Chicago Tribune claims his attention. But it has been enough for me to feel like he's a dad.

My mother is increasingly a take-charge person and Dad's bastion of support through ever-increasing career stresses. Mom, in turn, runs the household and Christmas continues to be her domain for many years.

Both times, in my childhood, when Dad wrenches my heart with his anger at me, centered on relationships with people. Our eventual simpatico and understanding would be grounded in our reliance on spirituality. It is our reliance on something bigger than ourselves that helps us forgive and simply love each other.

"Who sits next to you in your new class?" It is a winter evening in 1967; we've lived in Battle Creek just a short time. I am 10. This is the second time Dad loses his temper with me. Dad, in shirt, suit coat and tie, asks me this from the head of the dining room table. It is a weeknight, and I can only surmise that he has brought a visiting salesman—a protégée—home for dinner, because we are eating in the dining room.

This is a rare show of interest by Dad into my day-to-day life, and I feel a warmth spreading inside me.

"His name is Ron, he lives on Capital Avenue and he rides my bus," I spew forth with my plethora of information. "And guess what else? He's Catholic, but he's really nice." I smile, so pleased to let Mom and Dad know that Catholics really are OK . All my 10 years of life, Baba has lamented the Catholic faith. While he has no specific complaint against this branch of Christianity, he talks about "all the Catholics," in the same vein he disparages unions, and "coloreds."

There is, at that point, a single, short burst of anger from Dad. "Why?" he says, his fist clenching his fork, "would you say that?"

"I dunno," I mumble.

What I want to say is, "cause Baba says he doesn't like Catholics and 'cause you and Mom said the MacGregors next door to us in Winnetka had too many kids, and that Catholics just go to church so they can confess and then feel OK about everything."

But I keep quiet because I am scared. I'm not scared that he will hit me; Dad never hits me. But maybe if I say something else, he doesn't like, he won't do all the stuff he's supposed to do, like make a lot of money.

"Don't upset your dad," Mom always says.

I don't really know what will happen if we—me and Robbie and Betsy—upset him a lot. Something really bad, I guess. Like when I was nine, I have learned not to share my new thoughts with Dad because if they cause self-revelations that he is uncomfortable with, he will get really mad at me.

My dad is not prone to fits of anger, or yelling. He will yell only a few times as Rob becomes a teenager and becomes increasingly frustrated with Dad. My dad's unwillingness to try to understand—let alone respect—Rob's tremendous talent in rebuilding motors and engines, usually in a side yard shed Dad prefers be kept meticulous, results in a major fight. The two will erupt at each other, when I am 13, and Rob is 16. I will run from the house when this happens.

"Well, Beaver, I feel quite a bit of blame for all of this,"

Ward to Beaver, "Beaver and Ivanhoe," season 3, episode 36.

"You know, I'm not going to know what to say to him," Ward to June. "I suppose he'll hate us for it all, and I don't blame him."

Ward to June, "Party Invitation," season 1, episode 15.

"Well, there's only one thing to do. I've got to go upstairs and tell them I made a mistake. I've just to tell them I flew off the handle and made a fool of myself."

Ward to June, "Beaver's Bad Day," season 1, episode 34.

When I am 31 years old, I just want Dad to care enough about me to get angry. I return home every Christmas until I am married, at 33. By my early 30s, my Noyes grandparents are dead, my cousins are scattered and the Christmas Eve gathering we try to all recreate in my great-aunt's apartment is forlorn, only a handful of us still around to gather.

This year, on Christmas day, I awake in my parents' Barrington home, a house they have recently moved to and so perfectly decorated I can't fall asleep in the guest bedroom where the climbing flower wallpaper matches the shelf paper in the antique bureau drawers, and the antiques scream of the WASPish expectations of generations past. I have returned for a long weekend from Vermont, where I am feeling settled. Dad is a year away from retiring; I know little of the long hours he is logging to make sure his business is a success. He doesn't talk of the commute he has on congested Chicago tollways, and I don't ask him. Too, he probably feels a bit at odds, with Betsy and Rob married and in their own homes.

I am just months away from my discovery that I need only to love myself before I can ask Dad if he loves me. That four-word question still hangs between us, unspoken, like a blackout curtain that simply won't be lifted.

It is a bright, blustery uncustomary sunny December 25, and I rise expecting that the three of us will share a morning of no "should's or must-do's" before my brother's family arrives for dinner.

Dad is outside that Christmas morning. I see his blob of red ski parka from the kitchen window and as I sip my coffee, I ask Mom what he is doing. She is buttering rolls and wrapping them in foil.

"Stacking wood," she says. "He already ate but I thought we'd have brunch in a couple of hours."

A storm three days earlier has felled large trees and crews have sawed them and left the pile of logs in a disheveled, every-which-way pile. I don my red running tights and running shoes and a sweatshirt. I pull a pair of bright yarn mittens out of a bag of hats and mittens Mom has kept.

It does not occur to me that Dad would spend Christmas—the one day he has always suspended reality—stacking logs until the job is done. I offer to help a bit before I run, but thirty minutes into the job when I turn away to go running, Dad says the job isn't done yet.

"How long do you plan to work?" I ask.

"Till it's done," he responds. He doesn't look up and he doesn't explain, as Tim will years later, that a mind-numbing, physical task is often the ticket to letting go of the uncontrollable elements of a demanding job, and that my help, and my camaraderie could make the job fun.

Yes, now I get that stacking an unsightly pile of logs was for him cathartic and a stress-buster from his days of selling forklift trucks and balancing ledgers and mediating disputes. But what explodes insides me at that moment is red, angry, huge, combustible, scary and yet, deep down, almost calming.

"You," I scream at Dad—the very first and only time in my life I remember screaming at him—"are going to be a lonely old man."

I turn; I run to the house and scream the same message into Mom about my father, and run seven miles on frozen, snow-covered roads.

I think I hate this man.

CHAPTER SEVENTEEN
"NEVER BE THE SAME"

"Go now, knowing you can never be the same again."
I need spirituality.

A square patch of sunlight lands on a pew at the Williston Federated Church on a February Sunday morning. It hits the far-right side of the pew; it is where I always try to sit. I'm a sun worshiper; I'd chosen Vermont as a place to live without thinking of the sunnier climes of the West. This small, white-steepled Methodist church is my refuge, often, for the two years I live with Amy. I gain a great deal from it—far more than I give back—and on some of the most frigid weekends of these winters, it might be the only time I venture outside.

I had entered this church less than twenty-four hours after Amy picked me up from my People Express flight in July of 1986. I have no car; she is driving me, the next day, to a fiction writing workshop at Bennington College. I will fly back to Chicago later in the summer, buy a car and collect my leavings in my parents' basement.

During the month I spend at Bennington College, I go to classes and author readings and, sitting at the small desk in a single room in my dormitor, typing away, revising and "finishing" my, in-my-mind-soon-to-be-bestseller article, about my first falling in love. It is a trite, wound-opening piece that I think I have to write; it garners flat, snickering-like comments when I read it aloud in class, and with those comments, I let my hopes deflate. At the workshop's end, my assigned professor/mentor simply suggests I go to graduate school for an MFA if I want to be a successful writer.

Now, thirty-five years later, I realize how invaluable that experience was, but at the time it results in my returning to Williston, defeated in my author dreams. Even with my savings to live on, I have no hope I will be successful simply "writing," and immediately turn to job hunting. In retrospect, all I really wanted was to find a new tribe of people—professionally and socially—so I would feel I belonged.

The Williston Federated Church helps anchor me.

I have a spiritual community in Chicago, at the rambling Fourth Presbyterian Church on Michigan Avenue and I will have that community in Williston and later at the Episcopal Church in Essex Junction. I have that faith now at the First Congregational Church in Essex Junction, and I sometimes seek a life ring so strong that I wonder if I am asking too much.

Yet it is never too much, and it is spirituality that finally lets me accept that Dad loves me.

I am not sure then exactly what I am seeking from church. Reliance on a spiritual being? Socialization? An hour a week to stop, sit still and listen? Intellectual stimulation? I leave the small neighborhood Methodist church after a few months and try out a socially-progressive Protestant church on the University of Vermont campus. I burn out on the long list of social causes the members support, and leave every Sunday feeling guilty. So I am drawn back to the church a few miles down the road from Amy's house, and treat the hour on Sunday mornings there as a meditative retreat. I struggle, too, during this time with making decisions. Dad made decisions with confidence and I think I am supposed to, but I do not. For an anxious person, second-guessing a decision is just like putting on that well-worn, comfortable pair of jeans. It feels so good, and so right, to question yourself and sap the energy of those close to you by seeking their affirmation.

I hear a story from a friend that his parents made their decision on their purchase of a summer cabin, when he was three years old, because they were looking at the properties by boat, and he was getting sea sick on the choppy waters. The cabin for sale where the realtor docked the boat, the parents said, would do just fine. Their son was not feeling well, and it was time to go home. They were meant to buy this cabin, they said. My dad, while decisive and confident, makes such decisions based on facts. I have to learn, as an adult, to factor emotions into my decisions; I still struggle with this.

A year into living with Amy, I am at the busiest point of my freelancing. A steady source of jobs, and thus income, is a small, private Catholic college in Burlington. The public relations department of this now-defunct college is, at the time, churning out brochures, press releases and magazines. How ironic that, six months into working with the college, a middle-aged female administrator feels I don't do justice to an interview with honor students and decides, unequivocally, that my services are no longer needed.

Like my dismissal at MacNeal Hospital two years earlier, I am presumed guilty and pushed out the door. I don't try to defend myself; I don't know how. It is a time when I am sleep deprived; I have been working full time, temporarily, at a weapons manufacturing company editing instruction manuals written by engineers, while still writing for the college, and other clients, evenings and weekends.

It is not the first, nor the last, time I will be told, by a woman, to leave a job.

I cannot work for women, and it will take me until I am 50 years old to face that handicap. Happily, I do face it and grow, and thrive working for women the last 15 years of my career.

But when I lose the work with the college—and with it income and a sense of belonging—I am miserable, anxious, and reeling from the loss of a steady client. I am also expecting far too much from a man I am dating and from Amy, whom I learn years later has insurmountable problems in sharing her emotions.

One Sunday afternoon, in February, I help chaperone a group of high school kids from the church to go ice skating on a frozen lake in Williston. It is a day of frigid temps, and windy, and I think how glad I am to have a reason to be outside. It is too cold for me to ski, and I think that these kids need me—that I am part of something, and it dawns on me that really, this is all I want. We start a bonfire, and I feel warmth, and belonging. Two weeks later, we take the kids to a small, truck-operated ski hill, just minutes from the church. It is a Sunday afternoon, and we all take multiple runs down the small hill, tucked in the shadow of a farm. I gather the kids in the small shelter at the end.

"I feel like God is here," I venture to say to the half dozen kids. "And like he cares, and we all care about each other."

I don't recall how, or even if, the kids responded to me. I do remember eyes rolling. All I remember is the sense of belonging, of community, of caring.

I want to know that people count on me; I want to know that Dad counts on me.

But no one, I feel, cares.

The following Saturday is one of those not-really-winter, chilly, windy, frozen-slush-on-the-ground days. It's a clean-the-closets, go-to-a-movie or curl-up-on-the-couch-with-a-book-day. I choose to sit on my bed and suddenly I can't stop crying. I try to take a walk, and a freezing rain begins, so it is back in the house.

Amy has gone out, when I return from my brief attempt at a walk. I go up to my room; I wonder how I'll lift myself out of this nearly smothering quicksand. I can keep getting sucked down, or start the uphill climb.

God saves me.

The next morning, I am in the same spot at church halfway back on the right side, right where the sunlight filters in through, what I truly believe were emerald green and bright blue stained-glass windows. I recall the sun creating beautiful hues of blues and greens that morning, but when

I return to the church 32 years later and really look around. I see the windows are clear glass.

I ask a longtime member. Had they been stained glass windows in 1987?

"No," she replies. "But all that matters is that that is how you remember them."

That morning in 1987, I watch the minister's bearded head move with the gesticulations of an excited man. He is short with brown hair, middle-aged with eyes that emit light and friendliness. I listen from my sentry in the sunshine. But my mind is clogged with questions. Does Amy really want me living in her house? Why am I a wreck with dating? How will I find more clients?

"Go now," Rev. William Cotant says from the back of the church. His message jolts me alert. This is a change from his customary final blessing. *"Go now, knowing you can never be the same again,"* he says.

I am jolted.

Not being the same again; forgiving, letting go? Way too scary.

But Rev. Cotant's words are out, and I have to own them. I have to change. Perhaps he had said those same words before and I hadn't been ready to hear them.

Now, I am ready. I have to be because I don't like this deep, dark hole I slid down the day before.

Rev. Cotant's words that morning wrap around me like my yellow "ni-ni," a scratchy wool blanket that I, as an infant and toddler with extreme dermatitis, for some inexplicable reason find comforting. Mom puzzles over my inseparable bond with this abrasive square of fabric because I always want soft cotton clothing and fret inconsolably if she dresses me in anything else. I think the "ni-ni " relieves stress when I am young because I find its silky binding such a comfort, contrasted with the rough woolly blanket.

I've got to stop wondering if my dad loves me.

From that day on, I receive unconditional love from Dad because, I suppose, I stop wondering about it. It is just there. I accept that God loves me; with that freedom and security I can simply love and I can let others love me. I am forced to forgive, convinced by God to let go of Dad's insensitivities, insecurities and failings. I begin to see the peace-loving, nature-centered, dedicated hard-working man that my Dad is. I ask for Dad's unconditional love and receive it.

I learn to love the man my father really is; a man who simply could not say "I love you," comfortably and confidently.

Dad gives me what I want, once I ask. He gives me his unconditional love.

CHAPTER EIGHTEEN
"TIM"

And, finally, I can love.

What a liberation, to know that I am loved by Dad—have always been loved even though he couldn't express it—and that by accepting God's love, I can feel my dad's love. I've freed myself from an emotional prison, really, one that I had been locked in far too long. When I acknowledge God's love, I also know I will be OK, no matter what happens to me.

This is freedom. This is living life with permission to pursue what makes you happy.

This will sustain me through the untimely, and sudden death of my best friend Amy, some 26 years later, a loss I will never comprehend.

And, when I discover God's unconditional love, my priorities for my life become clear.

I am 32 years old; I would like a life partner, and I want to be a mom; to love, nurture, and help my very own children grow. And, so, Dad's words from three years ago echo in my mind as I give myself permission to fall in love with a man I really, truly want to be with.

No more just trying to find out how many cute guys I can

attract, just to prove to myself I am desirable and capable of being loved.

"There's ways to be organized about this Emily," Dad had said, not unkindly, as he dropped me at the commuter train station in Barrington, one day when I had been spending the night at their house. This was three years before my move to Vermont. "If you spend more time with people you're compatible with, you're bound to meet single men you'd enjoy more." He suggested I join a dating service. He is intrigued by the radio ads he has heard, and is a strong advocate of meeting goals in measurable steps, efficiently, counting on reliable professionals to help you.

"Thanks, Dad, but don't need that," I'd mumbled in my seven a.m. sleep-fogged mind, wondering who in the world would succumb to such an organized approach to meeting a life partner. Adult life is organized enough, I'd thought, with work deadlines, bosses, expected ways to dress, paying bills. My personal life—my journey of creating a home and, ideally, family—should be like the John Lennon song I blast every Saturday morning, "Beautiful Boy," "Life is what happens to you while you're busy making other plans."

I wonder now what Dad thought of my response on that frigid winter morning? Did he mull it over as he pulled away from the train station and joined the flow of traffic toward his 30-minute commute? Did he worry about me? Or did his thoughts turn to the day of sales calls ahead?

In Vermont, I enroll in a $350 dating service, Compatibles, the only dating service in Burlington.

The owner meets with me in her small, windowless office. I don't believe she even took a photo of me. We simply filled out a questionnaire; she looks it over and interviews me, and I leave after an hour with the assurance of hearing from her. My personality, and desires in a partner, are encapsulated in one of her manila files.

It is her job to "match" profiles from the file cabinet behind her desk. She calls me with a description of the man she feels is a match, and, if I give permission, she then calls him and tells him about me. This is 1988; the man must make the call to the woman for a date.

There are disastrous dates (for me, anyway); dates in which my hopes will be lifted, only to be trod upon, and depressing dates. It is, for me, much like job interviewing. After phone calls, you gear yourself up to be high energy, make an effort to look and feel your best, and meet the prospect. I learn, quickly, to suggest dates for a five p.m. beer or a weekend lunch. My first date, Bill, has suggested a Saturday evening of drinks, dinner and a movie. I bail out on the movie, not even concerned about my excuse. "Just can't eat," he says, looking up from his plate and glancing at me, shyly. I'd finished half my meal. "I've never eaten in front of a date before."

I met Chip, who lived two hours away in New Hampshire. We meet for lunch on the Saturday after Thanksgiving. Sunday evening, he calls to chat and ask if he could visit me the following weekend. I give an excuse of being busy. Tuesday morning, he calls at 7 a.m. to ask me to take a week-long trip to the Bahamas, the week between Christmas and New Year's.

"I'll pay," he says. "We could really have fun."

I suspect we all followed the dating service rules of no

follow-up phone calls once a second date was rejected, because Chip, fortunately, never calls again.

Then there was a week of waiting for the phone to ring after Chris, who travels for business, tells me on a Saturday lunch date that "I think I really want to ask you" to an office Christmas party, to take place in a week. No phone call. And then a date with a man who can only talk about his loneliness for his ex-wife and kids. This prompts a call to the dating service owner and a request for slightly better screening.

So, then Tim calls me, on a Sunday evening, December 18.

"It's Goo-jacque," Tim says on the phone, as he tries to tell me how to pronounce his last name, Guziak. I am on the phone in the bedroom of my condo, cradling the receiver under my chin as I wrap Christmas gifts on my bed.

"Oh, like Larry Lujack, the DJ in Chicago?" I ask.

"Yeah, kinda."

We discover we both went to high school in Michigan, about one hundred miles away from each other. We both have older siblings (he also has younger) and we both love the Great Lakes, and are equally in love with the Green Mountains.

"My four-year-old niece likes slugs," Tim says as I open the front door of my condo the next evening to this good-looking, brown-haired man with a crinkly smile. "Do you think she'll like this book?" He holds up a picture book with brightly crayoned-drawings of slugs in various forms, opening to a spread of a particularly gruesome-looking insect. It is cold outside. I laugh, out loud, and welcome him in.

Was he as nervous as I, unwilling to really relax and believe that this brief "date"—a meeting, really—might be a success?

"Stay for dinner," I suggest impulsively just a short time later. "I just have to run upstairs and change—I'm going out in a half hour—but I can make some eggs."

I am captured by his sense of humor, and I wonder if I will see him again. It is a week before Christmas and both of us plan to leave town by week's end.

I call him Wednesday evening. He had told me he was leaving town on Thursday to spend a week in Michigan with his family. We meet for lunch the next day at a pizza spot midway between our jobs. I hand him a small package wrapped in bright red Christmas paper. It is a small gift I picked out the evening before, because I want him to know a bit more about me.

"Oh… could be kinda interesting," Tim says, laughing when he sees he has unwrapped a cassette tape with then Burlington, VT Mayor Bernie Sanders' album "We Shall Overcome." I know nothing of Tim's political leanings, but I want him to know I am open to this progressive mayor.

Tim tells me later he listened only briefly to the tape. But our fledgling relationship survived the gift.

"It's the dog catcher, in Vermont." My mom picks up the phone a week later in their home in Barrington where I am visiting for a week. I flew to Chicago on December 24 for a week. She looks at me, quizzically. "He says he needs to speak to you."

The "dog catcher," who had generously offered on our second date to pick up my dog from the kennel in Burlington and watch him, asks me out for New Year's Eve. On that evening, our first real date, I fall in love.

Tim and I plunge into our relationship. I know that Tim is smart, ambitious and caring. I give myself permission—for the first time in seven years—to let my feelings go. He is most fun when we are outside. "Go for rad points,' Tim says as we ski off the cross country trails in the undeveloped forest near his house. I am living in a condo in Burlington, and his small contemporary A-frame is a weekend escape. I am beginning to love this man, I realize, as he accepts my passion for writing, and my strong independence. He brings out the best in me.

I believe I never would have met Tim, if I hadn't made peace with Dad. I had to accept Dad, and who he was, before I could love myself, or any man, completely. With the acceptance of Dad's shortcomings—hearing him say he loves me is a huge hurdle—I realize that I'd been loved all along.

It is a quick courtship, and our engagement in May feels right, and exciting. We plan a wedding in Vermont for September, and we are launched by family and friends into marriage and begin the journey.

Dad cries when I get married in 1989. Three years later we have our last really active day together. He is 70; I am 36, and we canoe—just the two of us—for an afternoon.

"Dad, do men ever get the weepies?" Beaver asks his Dad. "I don't know Beaver, but I wouldn't be surprised."

"Beaver's House Guest," season 4, episode 2.

Dad is struck by a neurological complication five months later, which will never be clearly diagnosed. For two months, he can't communicate clearly, or walk. He recovers and lives for 18 more years. For a few years, he regains some of his strength and is able to bike ride, play golf and drive a car. But his abilities decrease as he suffers from several strokes and, just weeks shy of 88 years old, he passes away.

He continues to anchor us, as best he can, during those 18 years of gradual decline. He tells all of us he loves us, time and again. He flies kites and reads stories with his grandchildren, shares readily of his wealth, and writes them letters.

Dad loved me and my siblings completely and wholly.

I just needed permission to accept and acknowledge his love.

Would my anxiety have been less had Dad been able to hug me, to say "I love you," or even asked me my favorite color? If I hadn't found the strength to acknowledge that as a Christian, I must forgive people; that I had to accept that Dad did the best he could?

I don't know.

But I do know to Just Ask for love. However you can.

AFTERWORD

Loving and nurturing your children is a fine line; it is this precarious dance where you want them to know they are the most important thing in your life, yet they are individuals and they have the means to go out and live their lives just the way they want to. You want to love them but not smother them; guide them and help them, yet empower them to know they can make their own decisions; that they carry within themselves the confidence and self-reliance to make their own way. You want them to know they are loved, and that they can live their lives absolutely however they want to, and your love for them will not change.

I did not know that.

I need the support of God to go forward with that. I need to know that there is something that will never go away, no matter what. Because people die or people leave you because they change. But God doesn't.

I tell my husband, on a walk a few years ago, that were he to unexpectedly and suddenly die, I would be OK. I tell him this because I am trying to illustrate how strong my faith is. What I mean to say is, 'I would be devastated if I ever lose you. But I would be OK because I have God.'

I hope he understands this; that my love for God simply

is my lifeline—that I was born with anxiety; that I was raised with a dad who didn't express himself, and that it is through my spirituality I have learned to live with my fears, my losses, my regrets.

And that I believe people just need to ask for what they want.

About the Author

Emily Thayer Guziak is a native Midwesterner who enjoys learning everyone's life story. Writing her first story at four years old, after watching the 1960 Kennedy-Nixon debate with her parents, Emily has been a journalist since 1978. She and her husband have raised three children. Now retired, Emily is passionate about writing, hiking and biking with family and friends, and creating community (especially when it involves her neighbor's desserts!) This is her first book.